Electronic Commerce

The Strategic Perspective

Electronic Commerce

The Strategic Perspective

Richard T. Watson

Terry College of Business
The University of Georgia

Pierre Berthon

School of Management
University of Bath

Leyland F. Pitt

Cardiff Business School
University of Wales

George M. Zinkhan

Terry College of Business
The University of Georgia

The Dryden Press
A Division of Harcourt College Publishers
Fort Worth • Philadelphia • San Diego • New York • Austin • Orlando • San Antonio
Toronto • Montreal • London • Sydney • Tokyo

Publisher: Michael Roche
Senior Acquisitions Editor: Bill Schoof
Marketing Manager: Lisé Johnson
Developmental Editors: Rebecca Linnenburger, Jana Pitts
Project Editor: John Haakenson
Production Manager: Angela Williams Urquhart
Art Director: Scott Baker

ISBN: 0-03-026533-9
Library of Congress Catalog Card Number: 99-63988

Address for Orders:
The Dryden Press, 6277 Sea Harbor Drive, Orlando, FL 328876777. 1-800-782-4479

Address for Editorial Correspondence:
The Dryden Press, 301 Commerce Street, Suite 3700, Fort Worth, TX 76102

Web site Address:
http://www.harcourtcollege.com

Printed in the United States of America

9 0 1 2 3 4 5 6 7 8   039   9 8 7 6 5 4 3 2
The Dryden Press
Harcourt College Publishers

To our families

Preface

Since 1995, the four of us have had a very active program of research on electronic commerce. We have published more than 20 refereed articles on this topic and have collectively given dozens of seminars on electronic commerce in more than 20 countries for a wide range of corporations and universities. We have tested and refined our ideas by working with corporations to develop electronic commerce strategies. The focus of our work has been to address fundamental issues that are common to many business practitioners. Thus, we have frequently emphasized the strategic elements of electronic commerce. In particular, we have explored the impact that Internet technology has on marketing strategy and practice. We have reflected on the feedback provided by many who have attended our seminars, workshops, and classes, and commented on our publications. As a result, we have refined and honed our thinking, and this book represents the culmination of these efforts.

This book reports the results of our research. It is written both for practitioners and business students. Managers wishing to understand how electronic commerce is revolutionizing business will find that our comprehensive coverage of essential business issues (e.g., pricing and distribution) answers many of their questions. Advanced business students (junior, seniors, and graduate students) will find that the blend of academic structure and practical examples provides an engaging formula for learning.

The book's title reflects some key themes that we develop. First, we are primarily concerned with electronic commerce, which we define as using technology (e.g., the Internet) to communicate or transact with stakeholders (e.g., customers). Second, we discuss how organizations must change in order to take advantage of electronic commerce opportunities. In this sense, our book offers *the* strategic perspective (i.e., the best way to operate a successful business in the 21st century). Third, with the growing importance of the Internet and related technologies, organizations must take electronic commerce into account when they are creating strategic plans. Thus, electronic commerce is a strategic perspective that all firms must adopt, both in the present and in the future. In other words, an organization that does not explicitly consider electronic commerce as a strategic imperative is probably making a crucial error. Here, we focus primarily on the opportunities and tactics that can lead to success in the electronic marketplace.

We live in exciting times. It is a rare event for an economy to move from one form to another. We are participating in the transition from the industrial to the information age. We all have an opportunity to participate in this historic event. The extent to which you partake in this revolution is determined, in part, by your desire to facilitate change and your understanding of how the new economy operates. We hope this book inspires you to become an electronic commerce change agent and also provides the wherewithal to understand what can be changed and how it can be changed.

We are now in the second phase of our electronic commerce research. In the next few years, we will publish research on, among other things:

- the relationship between Web page complexity and communication effectiveness;
- development of an instrument (WebQual) to measure Web page quality;
- the impact of electronic commerce on the role of the CIO;
- branding and electronic commerce;
- a global study of leading edge practices in electronic commerce;
- understanding the structure of information age firms;
- new models of economic revolution as suggested by electronic commerce;
- motives of business individuals for creating Web sites.

We will update the book's accompanying Web site as we release this research. We intend to use the Web site to maintain the currency of this book.

Supplements

Accompanying this book is an extensive Web site[1] that provides:

- overhead slides in PowerPoint format;
- links to Web sites mentioned in the book and other useful sites;
- additional teaching material, such as teaching cases.

Acknowledgments

We thank the many people who have attended our presentations on electronic commerce. Their insightful comments have sharpened our analysis and provided many examples of how electronic commerce is altering the rules of business.

The support of Bill Schoof at Harcourt was much appreciated.

Good reading, good thinking, and enjoy the revolution.

---

1. http://www.harcourtcollege.com

Table of Contents

1

Electronic commerce: Introduction

Introduction

Electronic commerce is a revolution in business practices. If organizations are going to take advantage of new Internet technologies, then they must take a strategic perspective. That is, care must be taken to make a close link between corporate strategy and electronic commerce strategy.

In this chapter, we address some essential strategic issues, describe the major themes tackled by this book, and outline the other chapters. Among the central issues we discuss are defining electronic commerce, identifying the extent of a firm's Internet usage, explaining how electronic commerce can address the three strategic challenges facing all firms, and understanding the parameters of disintermediation. Consequently, we start with these issues.

Electronic commerce defined

Electronic commerce, in a broad sense, is the use of computer networks to improve organizational performance. Increasing profitability, gaining market share, improving customer service, and delivering products faster are some of the organizational performance gains possible with electronic commerce. Electronic commerce is more than ordering goods from an on-line catalog. It involves all aspects of an organization's electronic interactions with its stakeholders, the people who determine the future of the organization. Thus, electronic commerce includes activities such as establishing a Web page to support investor relations or communicating electronically with college students who are potential employees. In brief, **electronic commerce** involves the use of information technology to enhance communications and transactions with all of an organization's stakeholders. Such stakeholders include customers, suppliers, government regulators, financial institutions, mangers, employees, and the public at large.

Who should use the Internet?

Every organization needs to consider whether it should have an Internet presence and, if so, what should be the extent of its involvement. There are two key factors to be considered in answering these questions.

First, how many existing or potential customers are likely to be Internet users? If a significant proportion of a firm's customers are Internet users, and the search costs for the product or service are reasonably (even moderately) high, then an organization should have a presence; otherwise, it is missing an opportunity to inform and interact with its customers. The Web is a friendly and extremely convenient source of information for many customers. If a firm does not have a Web site, then there is the risk that potential customers, who are Web savvy, will flow to competitors who have a Web presence.

Second, what is the information intensity of a company's products and services? An information-intense product is one that requires considerable information to describe it completely. For example, what is the best way to describe a CD to a potential customer? Ideally, text would be used for the album notes listing the tunes, artists, and playing time; graphics would be used to display the CD cover; sound would provide a sample of the music; and a video clip would show the artist performing. Thus, a CD is information intensive; multimedia are useful for describing it. Consequently, Sony Music provides an image of a CD's cover, the liner notes, a list of tracks, and 30-second samples of some tracks. It also provides photos and details of the studio session.

The two parameters, number of customers on the Web and product information intensity, can be combined to provide a straightforward model (see Figure 1-1) for determining which companies should be using the Internet. Organizations falling in the top right quadrant are prime candidates because many of their customers have Internet access and their products have a high information content. Firms in the other quadrants, particularly the low-low quadrant, have less need to invest in a Web site.

Why use the Internet?

Along with other environmental challenges, organizations face three critical strategic challenges: demand risk, innovation risk, and inefficiency risk. The Internet, and especially the Web, can be a device for reducing these risks.

Demand risk

Sharply changing demand or the collapse of markets poses a significant risk for many firms. Smith-Corona, one of the last U.S. manufacturers of typewriters, filed for bankruptcy in 1995. Cheap personal computers destroyed the typewriter market. In simple terms, **demand risk** means fewer customers want to buy a firm's wares. The globalization of the world market and increasing

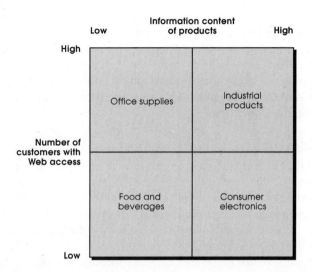

Figure 1-1. Internet presence grid with illustrative examples

deregulation expose firms to greater levels of competition and magnify the threat of demand risk. To counter demand risk, organizations need to be flexible, adaptive, and continually searching for new markets and stimulating demand for their products and services.

The **growth strategy matrix** [Ansoff, 1957] suggests that a business can grow by considering products and markets, and it is worthwhile to speculate on how these strategies might be achieved or assisted by the Web. In the cases of best practice, the differentiating feature will be that the Web is used to attain strategies that would otherwise not have been possible. Thus, the Web can be used as a **market penetration** mechanism, where neither the product nor the target market is changed. The Web merely provides a tool for increasing sales by taking market share from competitors, or by increasing the size of the market through occasions for usage. The U.K. supermarket group Tesco is using its Web site to market chocolates, wines, and flowers. Most British shoppers know Tesco, and many shop there. The group has sold wine, chocolates and flowers for many years. Tesco now makes it easy for many of its existing customers (mostly office workers and professionals) to view the products in a full-color electronic catalogue, fill out a simple order form with credit card details, write a greeting card, and facilitate delivery. By following these tactics, Tesco is not only taking business away from other supermarkets and specialty merchants, it is also increasing its margins on existing products through a premium pricing strategy and markups on delivery.

Alternatively, the Web can be used to **develop markets**, by facilitating the introduction and distribution of existing products into new markets. A presence on the Web means being international by definition, so for many firms with limited resources, the Web will offer hitherto undreamed-of opportunities to tap into global markets. Icelandic fishing companies can sell smoked salmon to the world. A South African wine producer is able to reach and communicate with wine enthusiasts wherever they may be, in a more cost effective way. To a large extent, this is feasible because the Web enables international marketers to overcome the previously debilitating effects of time and distance, negotiation of local representation, and the considerable costs of promotional material production costs.

A finer-grained approach to market development is to create a one-to-one customized interaction between the vendor and buyer. Bank America offers customers the opportunity to construct their own bank by pulling together the elements of the desired banking service. Thus, customers adapt the Web site to their needs. Even more advanced is an approach where the Web site is adaptive. Using demographic data and the history of previous interactions, the Web site creates a tailored experience for the visitor. Firefly markets technology for adaptive Web site learning. Its software tries to discover, for example, what type of music a visitor likes so that it can recommend CDs. Firefly is an example of software that, besides recommending products, electronically matches a visitor's profile to create virtual communities, or at least groups of like-minded people—virtual friends—who have similar interests and tastes.

Any firm establishing a Web presence, no matter how small or localized, instantly enters global marketing. The firm's message can be watched and heard by anyone with Web access. Small firms can market to the entire Internet world with a few pages on the Web. The economies of scale and scope enjoyed by large organizations are considerably diminished. Small producers do not have to negotiate the business practices of foreign climes in order to expose their products to new markets. They can safely venture forth electronically from their home base. Fortunately, the infrastructure—international credit cards (e.g., Visa) and international delivery systems (e.g., UPS)—for global marketing already exists. With communication via the Internet, global market development becomes a reality for many firms, irrespective of their size or location.

The Web can also be a mechanism that facilitates **product development**, as companies who know their existing customers well create exciting, new, or alternative offerings for them. *The Sporting Life* is a U.K. newspaper specializing in providing up-to-the-minute information to the gaming fraternity. It offers reports on everything from horse and greyhound racing to betting odds for sports ranging from American football to snooker, and from golf to soccer. Previously, the paper had been restricted to a hard copy edition, but the Web has given it significant opportunities to increase its timeliness in a time sensitive business. Its market remains, to a large extent, unchanged—bettors and sports enthusiasts in the U.K. However, the new medium enables it to do things that were previously not possible, such as hourly updates on betting changes in major horse races and downloadable racing data for further spreadsheet and statistical analysis by serious gamblers. Most importantly, *The Sporting Life* is not giving away this service free, as have so many other publishers. It allows prospective subscribers to sample for a limited time, before making a charge for the on-line service.

Finally, the Web can be used to **diversify** a business by taking new products to new markets. American Express Direct is using a Web site to go beyond its traditional traveler's check, credit card, and travel service business by providing on-line facilities to purchase mutual funds, annuities, and equities. In this case, the diversification is not particularly far from the core business, but it is feasible that many firms will set up entirely new businesses in entirely new markets.

Innovation risk

In most mature industries, there is an oversupply of products and services, and customers have a choice, which makes them more sophisticated and finicky consumers. If firms are to continue to serve these sophisticated customers, they must give them something new and different; they must innovate. Innovation inevitably leads to imitation, and this imitation leads to more oversupply. This cycle is inexorable, so a firm might be tempted to get off this cycle. However, choosing not to adapt and not to innovate will lead to stagnation and demise. Failure to be as innovative as competitors—**innovation risk**—is a second strategic challenge. In an era of accelerating technological development, the firm that fails to improve continually its products and services is likely to lose market share to competitors and maybe even disappear (e.g., the typewriter company). To remain alert to potential innovations, among other things, firms need an open flow of concepts and ideas. Customers are one viable source of innovative ideas, and firms need to find efficient and effective means of continual communication with customers.

Internet tools can be used to create open communication links with a wide range of customers. E-mail can facilitate frequent communication with the most innovative customers. A bulletin board can be created to enable any customer to request product changes or new features. The advantage of a bulletin board is that another customer reading an idea may contribute to its development and elaboration. Also, a firm can monitor relevant discussion groups to discern what customers are saying about its products or services and those of its competitors.

Inefficiency risk

Failure to match competitors' unit costs—**inefficiency risk**—is a third strategic challenge. A major potential use of the Internet is to lower costs by distributing as much information as possible electronically. For example,

Information sharing

A worldwide billion-dollar publishing company, Thompson Corporation, has been experiencing limited leverage because the business is so decentralized. Its various companies failed to share information on a regular basis, so that a single supplier can have multiple contracts, especially when many of the companies do not share the Thompson name.

With the introduction of an extranet initiated by the Thompson Optimized Purchasing Services (TOPS) team, the 1,200 users now have access to up-to-date information. Because the various companies do not share a common software infrastructure, the team decided to use Web browsers for sharing information.

To date, the TOPS program has contributed to $60 million (€55 million) in savings. It has reduced contract costs by 13 percent and helped suppliers reduce their costs as well, with some of these savings being passed on to Thompson companies.

TOPS is not a centralized purchasing service, and the various companies are not obliged to participate. Nonetheless, the extranet provides the companies with information that they did not previously have available.

Adapted from Sliwa, C. 1998. Extranet cuts purchase costs. *Computerworld*, Nov. 23, 45.

American Airlines now uses its Web site for providing frequent flyers an update of their current air miles. Eventually, it may be unnecessary to send expensive paper mail to frequent flyers or to answer telephone inquiries.

The cost of handling orders can also be reduced by using interactive forms to capture customer data and order details. Savings result from customers directly entering all data. Also, because orders can be handled asynchronously, the firm can balance its work force because it no longer has to staff for peak ordering periods.

Many Web sites make use of FAQs—frequently asked questions—to lower the cost of communicating with customers. A firm can post the most frequently asked questions, and its answers to these, as a way of expeditiously and efficiently handling common information requests that might normally require access to a service representative. UPS, for example, has answers to more than 40 frequent customer questions (e.g., What do I do if my shipment was damaged?) on its FAQ page. Even the FBI's 10 Most Wanted list is on the Web, and the FAQs detail its history, origins, functions, and potential.

Disintermediation

Electronic commerce offers many opportunities to reformulate traditional modes of business. **Disintermediation**, the elimination of intermediaries such as brokers and dealers, is one possible outcome in some industries. Some speculate that electronic commerce will result in widespread disintermediation, which makes it a strategic issue that most firms should carefully address. A closer analysis enables us to provide some guidance on identifying those industries least, and most, threatened by disintermediation.

Consider the case of Manheim Auctions.[1] It auctions cars for auto makers (at the termination of a lease) and rental companies (when they wish to retire a car). As an intermediary, it is part of a chain that starts with the car owner (lessor or rental company) and ends with the consumer. In a truncated value chain, Manheim and the car dealer are deleted. The car's owner sells directly to the consumer. Given the Internet's capability of linking these parties, it is not surprising that moves are already afoot to remove the auctioneer.

Edmunds, publisher of hard-copy and Web-based guides to new and used cars, is linking with a large auto-leasing company to offer direct buying to customers. Cars returned at the end of the lease will be sold with a warranty, and financing will be arranged through the Web site. No dealers will be involved. The next stage is for car manufacturers to sell directly to consumers, a willingness Toyota has expressed and that large U.S. auto makers are considering. On the other hand, a number of dealers are seeking to link themselves to customers through the Internet via the Autobytel Web site. Consumers contacting this site provide information on the vehicle desired and are directed to a dealer in their area who is willing to offer them a very low markup on the desired vehicle.

We gain greater insight into disintermediation by taking a more abstract view of the situation (see Figure 1-2). A value chain consists of a series of organizations that progressively convert some raw material into a product in the hands of a consumer. The beginning of the chain is 0_1 (e.g., an iron ore miner) and the end is O_n (e.g., a car owner). Associated with a value chain are physical and information flows, and the information flow is usually bi-directional. Observe that it is really a value network rather than a chain, because any organization may receive inputs from multiple upstream objects.

Consider an organization that has a relatively high number of physical inputs and outputs. It is likely this object will develop specialized assets for processing the physical flows (e.g., Manheim has invested heavily in reconditioning centers and is the largest non-factory painter of automobiles in the world). The need to process high volume physical flows is likely to result in economies of scale. On the information flow side, it is not so much the volume of transactions that matters since it is relatively easy to scale up an automated transaction

---

1. McKeown, P. G., and R. T. Watson. *Manheim Online.* Terry College, University of Georgia. Contact rwatson@uga.edu for a copy.

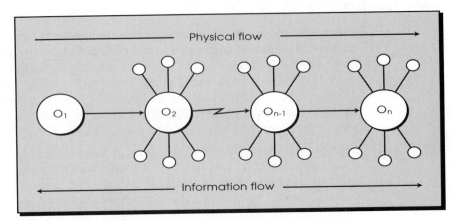

Figure 1-2. Value network

processing system. It is the diversity of the information flow that is critical because diversity increases decision complexity. The organization has to develop knowledge to handle variation and interaction between communication elements in a diverse information flow (e.g., Manheim has to know how to handle the transfer of titles between states).

Combining these notions of physical flow size and information flow diversity, we arrive at the disintermediation threat grid (see Figure 1-3). The threat to Manheim is low because of its economies of scale, large investment in specialized assets that a competitor must duplicate, and a well-developed skill in processing a variety of transactions. Car dealers are another matter because they are typically small, have few specialized assets, and little transaction diversity. For dealers, disintermediation is a high threat. The on-line lot can easily replace the physical lot.

We need to keep in mind that disintermediation is not a binary event (i.e., it is not on or off for the entire system). Rather, it is on or off for some linkages in the value network. For example, some consumers are likely to prefer to interact with dealers. What is more likely to emerge is greater consumer choice in terms of products and buying relationships. Thus, to be part of a consumer's options, Manheim needs to be willing to deal directly with consumers. While this is likely to lead to channel conflict and confusion, it is an inevitable outcome of the consumer's demand for greater choice.

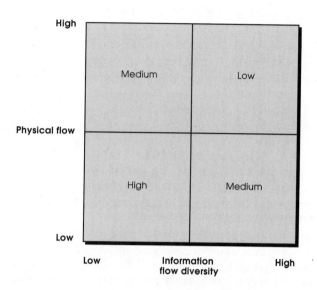

Figure 1-3. Disintermediation threat grid

Key themes addressed

Some of the key themes addressed in this book are summarized in Table 1-1. First, we introduce a number of new themes, models, metaphors, and examples to describe the business changes that are implied by the Internet. An example of one of our metaphors is Joseph Schumpeter's notion of **creative destruction**. That is, capitalist economies create new industries and new business opportunities. At the same time, these economies are destructive in that they sweep away old technologies and old ways of doing things. It is a sobering message that none of the major wagon makers was able to make the transition to automobile production. None of the manufacturers of steam locomotives became successful manufacturers of diesel locomotives. Will this pattern continue for the electronic revolution?

Amazon.com has relatively few employees and no retail outlets; and yet, it has a higher market capitalization than Barnes & Noble, which has more than one thousand retail outlets. Nonetheless, Barnes & Noble is fighting back by creating its own Web-based business. In this way, the Internet may spawn hybrid business strategies—those that combine innovative electronic strategies with traditional methods of competition. Traditional firms may survive in the twenty-first century, but they must adopt new strategies to compete. In this book, we introduce a variety of models for describing these new strategies, and we describe new ways for firms to compete by taking advantage of the opportunities that electronic commerce reveals.

Table 1-1: Key themes addressed by this book

I.	New models, theories, metaphors, and examples for describing electronic commerce and its impact on business and society
	a. New models for creating businesses (via the Internet)
	b. Hybrid models that combine Internet strategies with traditional business strategies
	c. New forms of human behavior (e.g., chat rooms, virtual communities)
	d. New forms of consumer behavior (e.g., searching for information electronically)
	e. Postmodernism and the Web
II.	Describing the reliability and robustness of the technology that underlies the Internet and its multi-media component (the Web)
III.	Describing how organizations can compete today, with an emphasis on outlining electronic commerce strategies and tactics
	a. The Internet creates value for organizations
	b. The Internet enhances consumers' life quality
IV.	Predicting the future, especially the impact of information technology on future business strategies and business forms (e.g., "Amazoning" selected industries)
V.	Describing technology trends that will emerge in the future
VI.	New ways of communicating with stakeholders and measuring communication effectiveness
VII.	Comparing and contrasting the Internet with other communication media (e.g., TV and brochures)
VIII.	Key features of the Internet which make it a revolutionary force in the economy (a force of creative destruction)
	a. Speed of information transfer and the increasing speed of economic transactions
	b. Time compression of business cycles
	c. The influence of interactivity
	d. The power and effectiveness of networks
	e. Opportunities for globalization and for small organizations to compete
IX.	The multi-disciplinary perspective that is necessary to comprehend electronic commerce and the changes it inspires in the economic environment. Here, we focus on three disciplinary approaches:
	a. Marketing, marketing research, and communication
	b. Management information systems
	c. Business strategy
X.	Elements that underlie effective Web pages and Web site strategy.
XI.	New kinds of human interactions that are enhanced by the Internet, such as:
	a. Electronic town hall meetings
	b. Brand communities (e.g., the Web page for Winnebago owners)
	c. Chat rooms
	d. Virtual communities
XII.	New marketing strategies for pricing, promoting, and distributing goods and services

At the same time that information technology has the potential to transform business operations, it also has the potential to transform human behaviors and activities. The focus of our book is business strategy; so we concentrate on those human activities (e.g., consumer behavior) that intersect with business operations. Some examples of consumer behaviors that we discuss include: virtual communities; enhanced information search via the Web; e-mail exchanges (e.g., word-of-mouth communications about products, e-mail messages sent directly to organizations); direct consumer purchases over the Web (e.g., buying flowers, compact disks, software). Of course, the Internet creates new opportunities for organizations to gather information directly from consumers (e.g., interactively). The Internet provides a *place* where consumers can congregate and affiliate with one another. One implication is that organizations can make use of these new consumer groups to solve problems and provide consumer services in innovative ways. For instance, software or hardware designers can create chat rooms where users pose problems. At the same time, other consumers will visit the chat room and propose suggested solutions to these problems.

Value to organizations is one of our themes. As described previously, organizations can create value via the Internet by improving customer service. The stock market value of some high technology firms is almost unbelievable. Consider the U.S. steel industry, which dominated the American economy in the late nineteenth century and the first half of the twentieth century. As of March 1999, the combined market capitalization of the 13 largest American steel firms (e.g., U.S. Steel and Bethlehem Steel) is approximately $6 billion (€5.5 billion), less than one-third the value of the Internet bookseller, Amazon.com. On most days, the market capitalization of Microsoft rises or falls by more than the market capitalization of the entire U.S. integrated steel industry. Firms such as Microsoft do not have extensive tangible assets, as the steel companies do. In contrast, Microsoft is a knowledge organization, and it is this knowledge (and ability to invent new technologies and new technological applications) that creates such tremendous value for shareholders.

At the same time, technology creates value for consumers. Some of this value comes in the form of enhanced products and services. Some of the value comes from more favorable prices (perhaps encouraged by the increased competition that the Internet can bring to selected industries). Some of the value comes in the form of enhanced (and more rapid) communications—communications between consumers and communications between organizations and consumers. In brief, the Internet raises quality of life, and it has the potential to perform this miracle on a global scale.

To date, the Internet has begun to make some big changes in the business practices in selected industries (see Table 1-2). For instance, electronic commerce has taken over 2.2 percent of the U.S. leisure travel industry. In the near future, the Internet has the potential to transform many other industries (see Table 1-3). For instance, the $71.6 billion (€69 billion) furniture business is a possibility. Logistics is a key for success in this industry. Consumers would expect timely delivery and a mechanism for rejecting and returning merchandise if it didn't meet expectations.

Table 1-2: E-markets[a]

Industry	E-market ($U.S. billions)	Total market ($U.S. billions)	E-market share (percent)	Key players
Leisure travel	7.8	351.4	2.2	Expedia Travelocity
Brokerage services (assets managed)	397.0	trillions	0.1	Charles Schwab E-Trade
PC hardware (consumer)	2.4	41.2	5.8	Dell Compaq
Books (consumer)	1.2	15.0	8.0	Amazon.com Barnes & Noble
Auto sales (referrals)	6.5	447.0	1.5	Auto-by-tel Major U.S.?

a. Source: Corcoran, E. 1999. On-line: Amazoned. *Forbes*, Mar. 22, 55

What is the future of electronic commerce? As in any field of human endeavor, the future is very difficult to predict. We describe the promise of electronic commerce. As reflected in the stock prices of e-commerce enterprises, the future of electronic commerce seems very bright indeed. In this book, we present some trends to come, by taking a business strategy approach.

Table 1-3: E-market possibilities[a]

Industry	Size of market ($U.S. billions)	E-sales (U.S. millions)[b]	Players
Drugstore products	153.6	509	drugstore.com PlanetRX
Furniture	71.6	319	
Music	13.7	374	CD Now
Shoes	20.4	100	
Hardware stores	14.6	139	

a. Source: Corcoran, E. 1999. On-line: Amazoned. *Forbes*, Mar 22, 55
b. 1999 estimates.

One way to try to understand the future of the Internet is by comparing it to other (communication) technologies that have transformed the world in past decades (e.g., television and radio). Another way to understand the Internet is to consider the attributes that make it unique. These factors include the following:

- the speed of information transfer and the increasing speed of economic transactions;
- the time compression of business cycles;
- the influence of interactivity;
- the power and effectiveness of networks;
- opportunities for globalization.

The Internet is complex. We adopt an interdisciplinary approach to study this new technology and its strategic ramifications. Specifically, we concentrate on the following three disciplines: management information systems, marketing, and business strategy. As described at the outset of this chapter, we show how the Internet is relevant for communicating with multiple stakeholder groups. Nonetheless, since we approach electronic commerce from a marketing perspective, we concentrate especially on consumers (including business consumers) and how knowledge about their perspectives can be used to fashion effective business strategies. We focus on all aspects of electronic commerce (e.g., technology, intranets, extranets), but we focus particular attention on the Internet and its multi-media component, the Web.

For a variety of reasons, it is not possible to present a single model to describe the possibilities of electronic commerce. For that reason, we present multiple models in the following chapters. Some firms (e.g., Coca-Cola) find it virtually impossible to sell products on the Internet. For these firms, the Internet is primarily an information medium, a place to communicate brand or corporate image. For other firms (e.g., Microsoft), the Internet is both a communication medium and a way of delivering products (e.g., software) and services (e.g., on-line advice for users). In brief, one business model cannot simultaneously describe the opportunities and threats that are faced in the soft drink and software industries. The following section provides more details about this book and the contents of the remaining chapters.

Outline for the book

This book contains nine chapters. Chapter Two briefly describes the technology that makes electronic commerce possible, while Chapter Three introduces the topic of Web strategy. The major functions of marketing are described in the next five chapters: Promotion (Chapter Four); Promotion and Purchase (Chapter Five); Distribution (Chapter Six); Service (Chapter Seven); and

Pricing (Chapter Eight). The final chapter takes a broader, societal perspective and discusses the influence of electronic commerce on society. More details about each chapter are provided in the following sections.

Chapter Two: The technology of electronic commerce

Chapter Two deals with the technology that underlies electronic commerce. Specifically, we discuss the methods that computers use to communicate with each other. We compare and contrast:

- the Internet (which is global in nature and has the potential to communicate with multiple stakeholder groups);

- the intranet (which focuses on internal communications within the organization—such as communication with employees);

- the extranet (which concentrates on exchanges with a specific business partner).

At present, the majority of electronic commerce concerns business-to-business relationships (see Figure 1-4) and is strongly linked to this last category (the extranet, where organizations can conduct exchanges with other channel members). Chapter Two also introduces the security issues associated with electronic commerce. Security is important both for organizations and for consumers.

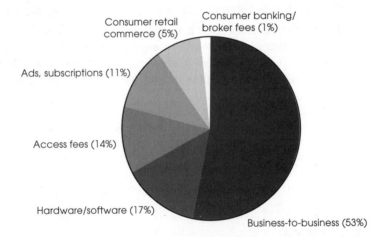

Figure 1-4. Electronic commerce estimates for 2001
(Source: Forrester Research in *New Media Magazine*, June 1998)

As the Internet is used to facilitate exchanges, it has the potential to create new forms of money (e.g., electronic money). When the Spanish conquistadors discovered the gold mines of the New World and transported that gold (and silver) back to their home country, the amount of currency in Europe expanded dramatically. The result was an economic boom across all of Western Europe. Similar periods of economic prosperity followed the expansion of the money supply that resulted from the popularization of checks and, later, credit cards. As new forms of money are created in cyberspace, a similar phenomenon may transpire. That is, the expanding money supply (through the acceptance of digital money) is another reason that electronic commerce has the potential to transform the modern economy in a way that benefits both consumers and business owners.

Chapter Three: Web strategy

This chapter introduces elements of electronic strategy. In particular, we describe business practices that evolve because of the way that the Web changes the nature of communication between firms and customers. We describe *attractors*, which firms use to draw visitors to their Web site, including sponsorship, the customer service center, and the town hall. We discuss different attractor strategies that are appropriate, depending upon what material an organization wants to put on the Web. We describe the strategies behind various services that organizations can provide in cyberspace.

Chapter Four: Promotion

This is the first of a series of five chapters that discuss the four major functions of marketing: promotion, price, distribution, and product (service). As the Web is a new communications medium, we devote two chapters to promotion. In Chapter Four, we introduce a model for thinking about communication strategy in cyberspace: the Integrated Internet Marketing model.

Chapter Five: Promotion and purchase

Chapter Five describes new methods for measuring communication effectiveness in cyberspace. Specifically, we discuss the Internet as a new medium, in contrast to broadcasting and publishing. Currently, Web users perceive this medium to be similar to a magazine, perhaps because 85 percent of Web content is text. Other capabilities of the Web (e.g., sound) are not extensively used at this point. In Chapter Five, we present several metaphors for thinking about what the Web can be, including the electronic trade show and the virtual flea market. We link the buying phases to Web functions and capabilities (such as identifying and qualifying prospects).

Measurement is a key theme in the chapter, so we describe the role of the Web in the marketing communications mix and introduce several formulas for measuring the success of Internet communications. Measurement of advertising effectiveness is a long-standing issue in marketing research. In some ways, this issue of communications effectiveness is almost impossible to answer. First, it is very difficult to isolate the effects of communication, independent from other important effects (such as changes in demand, price changes, distribution changes, or fluctuations in the economic environment). Second, there are likely to be important lagged effects that are difficult to isolate. For instance, a consumer might look at a Web page and then not use that information for making a purchase until six months later. However, the Web does create an environment where many new measures of communication effectiveness are possible. In the past, marketing research attempted to collect data about consumer attention levels in a very artificial way (e.g., by using information display boards). Now, it is possible to study click patterns and learn a lot about how consumers are processing organization-sponsored information.

Of course, the Web can be more than just a vehicle of communication. It can also serve as a medium for selling products and services. Two key measures that we describe in Chapter Five are: a) the ratio of purchasers to active visitors; and b) the ratio of repurchasers to purchasers. In certain circumstances, it is possible to collect direct behavioral measures about the effects of traditional advertising. On the Web, such behavioral measures are much more natural and much easier to collect on a routine basis.

Chapter Six: Distribution

In the nineteenth century, a shopkeeper was likely to know all of his customers by name. He knew their needs. In the late 1800s, organizations with a truly national presence (e.g., Standard Oil) began to dominate the economic landscape in the United States. This marked the birth of the large, modern corporation. Distribution problems became large and complex. Organizations needed to be large to respond to these logistical challenges. The advent of electronic commerce has the potential to transform logistics and distribution. Today, a small software firm in Austin, Texas, can deliver its product (via the Web) to a customer in Seoul, South Korea. The economic landscape is altered dramatically. This chapter (along with the others) is future oriented as we outline strategic directions that are likely to be successful in the twenty-first century.

Chapter Seven: Service

Services are more and more important in the U.S. economy. In Chapter Seven, we describe how electronic commerce comes to blur the distinction between products and services. Traditionally, services are a challenge to market because of four key properties: intangibility, simultaneity, heterogeneity, and perishability. In this chapter, we show how electronic commerce can be used to overcome traditional problems in services marketing.

Chapter Eight: Pricing

Price directly affects a firm's revenue. Chapter Eight describes pricing methods and strategies that are effective in cyberspace. We take a customer value perspective to illustrate various price-setting strategies (e.g., negotiation, reducing customer risk) and show how these strategies can be used to attain organizational objectives.

Chapter Nine: Postmodernism

The final chapter concentrates on societal changes that are encouraged by electronic commerce (and other related trends). Through the metaphors of modernism and postmodernism, we show how electronic commerce influences:

- perceptions of reality;
- notions of time and space;
- values;
- attitudes toward organizations.

Chapter Nine is future oriented and discusses electronic commerce as a revolutionary force that has the potential to transform society and transform consumers' perceptions of business practice.

The intrigues of introducing the intranet

The adoption of intranets in corporations has been at the expense of a number of in-house political battles and bargains. Although managers realize the many possible cost- and time-saving benefits of introducing an intranet, the corporate culture often has to change in the process.

Companies are slowly accepting the concept of sharing information with other departments. The security issues regarding publishing data and strategic documents are amplified because of concerns about hackers, although this is more an Internet problem.

Orstein, D. 1998. Fighting intranet flak. *Computerworld*, Nov. 23, 17.

Conclusion

As the prior outline clearly illustrates, this is a book about electronic commerce strategy. We focus on the major issues that challenge every serious thinker about the impact of the Internet on the future of business.

Cases

Dutta, S., and A. De Meyer. 1998. *E*trade, Charles Schwab and Yahoo!: the transformation of on-line brokerage*. Fontainebleau, France: INSEAD. ECCH 698-029-1.

Galal, H. 1995. *Verifone: The transaction automation company.* Harvard Business School, 9-195-088.

Vandermerwe, S., and M. Taishoff. 1998. *Amazon.com: marketing a new electronic go-between service provider*. London, U.K.: Imperial College. ECCH 598-069-1.

References

Ansoff, H. I. 1957. Strategies for diversification. *Harvard Business Review* 35 (2):113-124.

Child, J. 1987. Information technology, organizations, and the response to strategic challenges. *California Management Review* 30 (1):33-50.

Quelch, J. A., and L. R. Klein. 1996. The Internet and international marketing. *Sloan Management Review* 37 (3):60-75.

Zinkhan, G. M. 1986. Copy testing industrial advertising: methods and measure. In *Business marketing*, edited by A. G. Woodside. Greenwich, CT: JAI Press, 259-280.

2
Electronic commerce technology

Introduction

In the first chapter, we argued that organizations need to make a metamorphosis. They have to abandon existing business practices to create new ways of interacting with stakeholders. This chapter will provide you with the wherewithal to understand the technology that enables an organization to make this transformation.

Internet technology

Computers can communicate with each other when they speak a common language or use a common communication protocol. **Transmission Control Protocol/Internet Protocol** (TCP/IP) is the communication network protocol used on the Internet. TCP/IP has two parts. TCP handles the transport of data, and IP performs routing and addressing.

Data transport

The two main methods for transporting data across a network are circuit and packet switching. **Circuit switching** is commonly used for voice and package switching for data. Parts of the telephone system still operate as a circuit-switched network. Each link of a predetermined bandwidth is dedicated to a predetermined number of users for a period of time.

The Internet is a **packet switching** network. The TCP part of TCP/IP is responsible for splitting a message from the sending computer into packets, uniquely numbering each packet, transmitting the packets, and putting them together in the correct sequence at the receiving computer. The major advantage of packet switching is that it permits sharing of resources (e.g., a communication link) and makes better use of available bandwidth.

Routing

Routing is the process of determining the path a message will take from the sending to the receiving computer. It is the responsibility of the IP part of TCP/IP for dynamically determining the best route through the network. Because routing is dynamic, packets of the same message may take different paths and not necessarily arrive in the sequence in which they were sent.

Addressability

Messages can be sent from one computer to another only when every server on the Internet is uniquely addressable. The Internet Network Information Center (InterNIC) manages the assignment of unique IP addresses so that TCP/IP networks anywhere in the world can communicate with each other. An IP address is a unique 32-bit number consisting of four groups of decimal numbers in the range 0 to 255 (e.g., 128.192.73.60). IP numbers are difficult to recall. Humans can more easily remember addresses like aussie.mgmt.uga.edu. A Domain Name Server (DNS) converts aussie.mgmt.uga.edu to the IP address 128.192.73.60. The exponential growth of the Internet will eventually result in a shortage of IP addresses, and the development of next-generation IP (IPng) is underway.

Infrastructure

Electronic commerce is built on top of a number of different technologies. These various technologies created a layered, integrated infrastructure that permits the development and deployment of electronic commerce applications (see Figure 2-1). Each layer is founded on the layer below it and cannot function without it.

National information infrastructure

This layer is the bedrock of electronic commerce because all traffic must be transmitted by one or more of the communication networks comprising the national information infrastructure (NII). The components of an NII include the TV and radio broadcast industries, cable TV, telephone networks, cellular communication systems, computer networks, and the Internet. The trend in many countries is to increase competition among the various elements of the NII to increase its overall efficiency because it is believed that an NII is critical to the creation of national wealth.

Message distribution infrastructure

This layer consists of software for sending and receiving messages. Its purpose is to deliver a message from a server to a client. For example, it could move an HTML file from a Web server to a client running Netscape. Messages can be

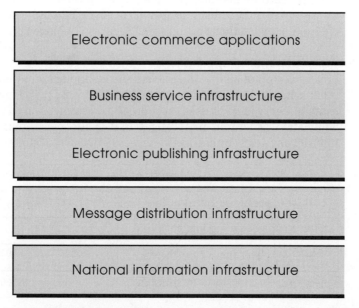

| Electronic commerce applications |
| Business service infrastructure |
| Electronic publishing infrastructure |
| Message distribution infrastructure |
| National information infrastructure |

Figure 2-1. Electronic commerce infrastructure

unformatted (e.g., e-mail) or formatted (e.g., a purchase order). Electronic data interchange (EDI), e-mail, and hypertext text transfer protocol (HTTP) are examples of messaging software.

Electronic publishing infrastructure

Concerned with content, the Web is a very good example of this layer. It permits organizations to publish a full range of text and multimedia. There are three key elements of the Web:

- A uniform resource locator (URL), which is used to uniquely identify any server;
- A network protocol;
- A structured markup language, HTML.

Notice that the electronic publishing layer is still concerned with some of the issues solved by TCP/IP for the Internet part of the NII layer. There is still a need to consider addressability (i.e., a URL) and have a common language across the network (i.e., HTTP and HTML). However, these are built upon the previous layer, in the case of a URL, or at a higher level, in the case of HTML.

Business services infrastructure

The principal purpose of this layer is to support common business processes. Nearly every business is concerned with collecting payment for the goods and services it sells. Thus, the business services layer supports secure transmission of credit card numbers by providing encryption and electronic funds transfer. Furthermore, the business services layer should include facilities for encryption and authentication (see "Security" on page 28).

Electronic commerce applications

Finally, on top of all the other layers sits an application. Consider the case of a book seller with an on-line catalog (see Figure 2-2). The application is a book catalog; encryption is used to protect a customer's credit card number; the application is written in HTML; HTTP is the messaging protocol; and the Internet physically transports messages between the book seller and customer.

Electronic commerce applications	*Book catalog*
Business services infrastructure	*Encryption*
Electronic publishing infrastructure	*HTML*
Message distribution infrastructure	*HTTP*
National information infrastructure	*Internet*

Figure 2-2. An electronic commerce application

Electronic publishing

Two common approaches to electronic publishing are Adobe's **portable document format (PDF)** and HTML. The differences between HTML and PDF are summarized in Table 2-1.

Table 2-1: HTML versus PDF

HTML	**PDF**
A markup language	A page description language
HTML files can be created by a wide variety of software. Most word processors can generate HTML	PDF files are created using special software sold by Adobe that is more expensive than many HTML creator alternatives
Browser is free	Viewer is free
Captures structure	Captures structure and layout
Can have links to PDF	Can have links to HTML
Reader can change presentation	Creator determines presentation

PDF

PDF is a **page description language** that captures electronically the layout of the original document. Adobe's Acrobat Exchange software permits any document created by a DOS, Macintosh, Windows, or Unix application to be converted to PDF. Producing a PDF document is very similar to printing, except the image is sent to a file instead of a printer. The fidelity of the original document is maintained—text, graphics, and tables are faithfully reproduced when the PDF file is printed or viewed. PDF is an operating system independent and printer independent way of presenting the same text and images on many different systems.

PDF has been adopted by a number of organizations, including the Internal Revenue Service for tax forms. PDF documents can be sent as e-mail attachments or accessed from a Web application. To decipher a PDF file, the recipient must use a special reader, supplied at no cost by Adobe for all major operating systems. In the case of the Web, you have to configure your browser to invoke the Adobe Acrobat reader whenever a file with the extension pdf is retrieved.

HTML

HTML is a **markup language**, which means it *marks* a portion of text as referring to a particular type of information.[1] HTML does not specify how this is to be interpreted; this is the function of the browser. Often the person using the browser can specify how the information will be presented. For instance, using the preference features of your browser, you can indicate the font and size for presenting information. As a result, you can significantly alter the look of the page, which could have been carefully crafted by a graphic artist to convey a particular look and feel. Thus, the you may see an image somewhat different from what the designer intended.

HTML or PDF?

The choice between HTML and PDF depends on the main purpose of the document. If the intention is to inform the reader, then there is generally less concern with how the information is rendered. As long as the information is readable and presented clearly, the reader can be given control of how it is presented. Alternatively, if the goal is to influence the reader (e.g., an advertisement) or maintain the original look of the source document (e.g, a taxation form or newspaper), then PDF is the better alternative. The two formats coexist. A PDF document can include links to a HTML document, and

---

1. For example, the HTML code '<b>Important</b>' is displayed as '**Important**' where the <b> and </b> tags turn bolding on and off, respectively.

vice versa. Also, a number of leading software companies are working on extensions to HTML that will give the creator greater control of the rendering of HTML (e.g., specifying the font to be used).

An on-line oil change

Car dealers are looking to retain customers through using new car maintenance software, which allows customers to schedule car services on-line. The software, Service Advisor Plus (developed by Interval Inc. and sold to dealers by Automotive Protection Corporation APCO), is designed to improve average service retention rates of 30 percent or lower (and even lower after warranties expire). Previously, some dealerships used phone calls or mail to give reminders to schedule services. The new software eliminates these costs.

The dealer pays a one-time fee of $1,000 (€910) to have details of the dealership, logo, Web site, and additional details loaded onto a CD, which is then copied and given to each customer. Customers use the Service Advisor Plus software on their PC, keying in their data, and then receive timely service reminders. A link to the dealer Web site is provided and appointments can be made. Discount coupons can also be printed.

Adapted from Wallace, B. 1999. Software will let customers book that oil change on-line. *Computerworld*, Feb. 8, 48.

Electronic commerce topologies

There are three types of communication networks used for electronic commerce (see Table 2-2), depending on whether the intent is to support cooperation with a range of stakeholders, cooperation among employees, or cooperation with a business partner. Each of these topologies is briefly described, and we discuss how they can be used to support electronic commerce.

Table 2-2: Electronic commerce topologies

Topology	Internet	Intranet	Extranet
Extent	Global	Organizational	Business partnership
Focus	Stakeholder relationships	Employee information and communication	Distribution channel communication

The **Internet** is a global network of networks. Any computer connected to the Internet can communicate with any server in the system (see Figure 2-3). Thus, the Internet is well-suited to communicating with a wide variety of stakeholders. Adobe, for example, uses its Web site to distribute software changes to customers and provide financial and other reports to investors.

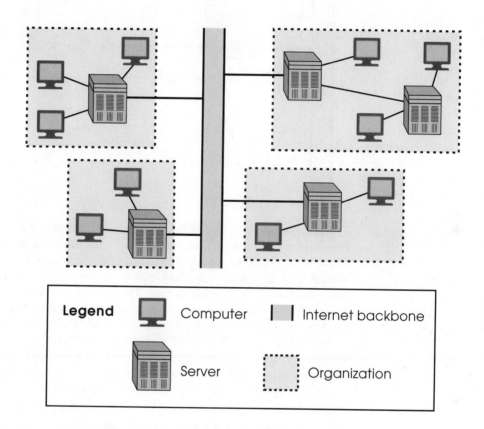

Figure 2-3. The Internet

Many organizations have realized that Internet technology can also be used to establish an intra-organizational network that enables people within the organization to communicate and cooperate with each other. This so-called **intranet** (see Figure 2-4) is essentially a fenced-off mini-Internet within an organization. A firewall (see page 29) is used to restrict access so that people outside the organization cannot access the intranet. While an intranet may not directly facilitate cooperation with external stakeholders, its ultimate goal is to improve an organization's ability to serve these stakeholders.

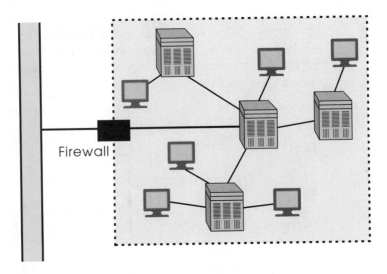

Figure 2-4. An Intranet

The Internet and intranet, as the names imply, are networks. That is, an array of computers can connect to each other. In some situations, however, an organization may want to restrict connection capabilities. An **extranet** (see Figure 2-5) is designed to link a buyer and supplier to facilitate greater coordination of common activities. The idea of an extranet derives from the notion that each business has a value chain and the end-point of one firm's chain links to the beginning of another's. Internet technology can be used to support communication and data transfer between two value chains. Communication is confined to the computers linking the two organizations. An organization can have multiple extranets to link it with many other organizations, but each extranet is specialized to support partnership coordination.

The economies gained from low-cost Internet software and infrastructure mean many more buyers and supplier pairs can now cooperate electronically. The cost of linking using Internet technology is an order of magnitude lower than using commercial communication networks for **electronic data interchange (EDI)**, the traditional approach for electronic cooperation between business partners.

EDI

EDI, which has been used for some 20 years, describes the electronic exchange of standard business documents between firms. A structured, standardized data format is used to exchange common business documents (e.g., invoices and shipping orders) between trading partners. In contrast to the free form of e-mail messages, EDI supports the exchange of repetitive, routine business transactions. Standards mean that routine electronic transactions can be

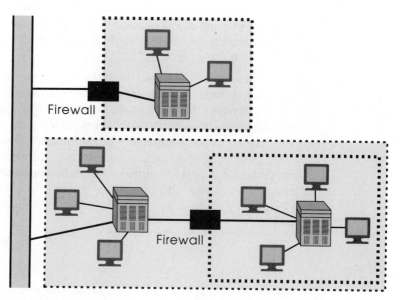

Figure 2-5. An extranet

concise and precise. The main standard used in the U.S. and Canada is known as ANSI X.12, and the major international standard is EDIFACT. Firms following the same standard can electronically share data. Before EDI, many standard messages between partners were generated by computer, printed, and mailed to the other party, that then manually entered the data into its computer. The main advantages of EDI are:

- paper handling is reduced, saving time and money;

- data are exchanged in real time;

- there are fewer errors since data are keyed only once;

- enhanced data sharing enables greater coordination of activities between business partners;

- money flows are accelerated and payments received sooner.

Despite these advantages, for most companies EDI is still the exception, not the rule. A recent survey in the United States showed that almost 80 percent of the information flow between firms is on paper. Paper should be the exception, not the rule. Most EDI traffic has been handled by value-added networks (VANs) or private networks. VANs add communication services to those provided by common carriers (e.g., AT&T in the U.S. and Telstra in Australia). However, these networks are too expensive for all but the largest 100,000 of the 6 million businesses in existence today in the United States. As a result, many businesses have not been able to participate in the benefits associated with EDI. However, the Internet will enable these smaller companies to take advantage of EDI.

Internet communication costs are typically less than with traditional EDI. In addition, the Internet is a global network potentially accessible by nearly every firm. Consequently, the Internet is displacing VANs as the electronic transport path between trading partners.

The simplest approach is to use the Internet as a means of replacing a VAN by using a commercially available Internet EDI package. EDI, with its roots in the 1960s, is a system for exchanging text, and the opportunity to use the multimedia capabilities of the Web is missed if a pure replacement strategy is applied. The multimedia capability of the Internet creates an opportunity for new applications that spawn a qualitatively different type of information exchange within a partnership. Once multimedia capability is added to the information exchange equation, then a new class of applications can be developed (e.g., educating the other partner about a firm's purchasing procedures).

Security

Security is an eternal concern for organizations as they face the dual problem of protecting stored data and transported messages. Organizations have always had sensitive data to which they want to limit access to a few authorized people. Historically, such data have been stored in restricted areas (e.g., a vault) or encoded. These methods of restricting access and encoding are still appropriate.

Electronic commerce poses additional security problems. First, the intent of the Internet is to give people remote access to information. The system is inherently open, and traditional approaches of restricting access by the use of physical barriers are less viable, though organizations still need to restrict physical access to their servers. Second, because electronic commerce is based on computers and networks, these same technologies can be used to attack security systems. Hackers can use computers to intercept network traffic and scan it for confidential information. They can use computers to run repeated attacks on a system to breach its security (e.g., trying all words in the dictionary for an account's password).

Access control

Data access control, the major method of controlling access to stored data, often begins with some form of visitor authentication, though this is not always the case with the Web because many organizations are more interested in attracting rather than restricting visitors to their Web site. A variety of authentication mechanisms may be used (see Table 2-3). The common techniques for the Internet are account number, password, and IP address.

Table 2-3: Authentication mechanisms

Class	Examples
Personal memory	Name, account number, password
Possessed object	Badge, plastic card, key, IP address
Personal characteristic	Fingerprint, voiceprint, signature, hand size

Firewall

A system may often use multiple authentication methods to control data access, particularly because hackers are often persistent and ingenious in their efforts to gain unauthorized access. A second layer of defense can be a **firewall**, a device (e.g., a computer) placed between an organization's network and the Internet. This barrier monitors and controls all traffic between the Internet and the intranet. Its purpose is to restrict the access of outsiders to the intranet. A firewall is usually located at the point where an intranet connects to the Internet, but it is also feasible to have firewalls within an intranet to further restrict the access of those within the barrier.

There are several approaches to operating a firewall. The simplest method is to restrict traffic to packets with designated IP addresses (e.g., only permit those messages that come from the University of Georgia—i.e., the address ends with uga.edu). Another screening rule is to restrict access to certain applications (e.g., Web pages). More elaborate screening rules can be implemented to decrease the ability of unauthorized people to access an intranet.

Implementing and managing a firewall involves a tradeoff between the cost of maintaining the firewall and the loss caused by unauthorized access. An organization that simply wants to publicize its products and services may operate a simple firewall with limited screening rules. Alternatively, a firm that wants to share sensitive data with selected customers may install a more complex firewall to offer a high degree of protection.

Coding

Coding or encryption techniques, as old as writing, have been used for thousands of years to maintain confidentiality. Although encryption is primarily used for protecting the integrity of messages, it can also be used to complement data access controls. There is always some chance that people will circumvent authentication controls and gain unauthorized access. To counteract this possibility, encryption can be used to obscure the meaning of data. The intruder cannot read the data without knowing the method of encryption and the key.

Societies have always needed secure methods of transmitting highly sensitive information and confirming the identity of the sender. In an earlier time, messages were sealed with the sender's personal signet ring—a simple, but easily forged, method of authentication. We still rely on personal signatures for checks and legal contracts, but how do you sign an e-mail message? In the information age, we need electronic encryption and signing for the orderly conduct of business, government, and personal correspondence.

Internet messages can pass through many computers on their way from sender to receiver, and there is always the danger that a sniffer program on an intermediate computer briefly intercepts and reads a message. In most cases, this will not cause you great concern, but what happens if your message contains your name, credit card number, and expiration date? The sniffer program, looking for a typical credit card number format of four blocks of four digits (e.g., 1234 5678 9012 3456), copies your message before letting it continue its normal progress. Now, the owner of the rogue program can use your credit card details to purchase products in your name and charge them to your account.

Without a secure means of transmitting payment information, customers and merchants will be very reluctant to place and receive orders, respectively. When the customer places an order, the Web browser should automatically encrypt the order prior to transmission—this is not the customer's task.

Credit card numbers are not the only sensitive information transmitted on the Internet. Because it is a general transport system for electronic information, the Internet can carry a wide range of confidential information (financial reports, sales figures, marketing strategies, technology reports, and so on). If senders and receivers cannot be sure that their communication is strictly private, they will not use the Internet. Secure transmission of information is necessary for electronic commerce to thrive.

Encryption

Encryption is the process of transforming messages or data to protect their meaning. Encryption scrambles a message so that it is meaningful only to the person knowing the method of encryption and the key for deciphering it. To everybody else, it is gobbledygook. The reverse process, decryption, converts a seemingly senseless character string into the original message. A popular form of encryption, readily available to Internet users, goes by the name of Pretty Good Privacy (PGP) and is distributed on the Web. PGP is a public domain implementation of public-key encryption.

Traditional encryption, which uses the same key to encode and decode a message, has a very significant problem. How do you securely distribute the key? It can't be sent with the message because if the message is intercepted, the key can be used to decipher it. You must find another secure medium for transmitting the key. So, do you fax the key or phone it? Either method is not completely secure and is time-consuming whenever the key is changed. Also, how do you know that the key's receiver will protect its secrecy?

A **public-key encryption** system has two keys: one private and the other public. A public key can be freely distributed because it is quite separate from its corresponding private key. To send and receive messages, communicators first need to create separate pairs of private and public keys and then exchange their public keys. The sender encrypts a message with the intended receiver's public key, and upon receiving the message, the receiver applies her private key (see Figure 2-6). The receiver's private key, the only one that can decrypt the message, must be kept secret to permit secure message exchange.

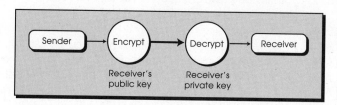

Figure 2-6. Encryption with a public-key system

The elegance of the public-key system is that it totally avoids the problem of secure transmission of keys. Public keys can be freely exchanged. Indeed, there can be a public database containing each person's or organization's public key. For instance, if you want to e-mail a confidential message, you can simply obtain the sender's public key and encrypt your entire message prior to transmission.

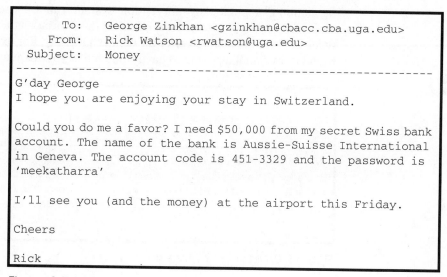

```
        To:    George Zinkhan <gzinkhan@cbacc.cba.uga.edu>
      From:    Rick Watson <rwatson@uga.edu>
   Subject:    Money
---------------------------------------------------------------
G'day George
I hope you are enjoying your stay in Switzerland.

Could you do me a favor? I need $50,000 from my secret Swiss bank
account. The name of the bank is Aussie-Suisse International
in Geneva. The account code is 451-3329 and the password is
'meekatharra'

I'll see you (and the money) at the airport this Friday.

Cheers

Rick
```

Figure 2-7. Message before encryption

Consider the message shown in Figure 2-7; the sender would hardly want this message to fall into the wrong hands. After encryption, the message is totally secure (see Figure 2-8). Only the receiver, using his private key, can decode the message.

```
       To:     George Zinkhan <gzinkhan@cbacc.cba.uga.edu>
     From:     Rick Watson <rwatson@uga.edu>
  Subject:     Money
------------------------------------------------------------
-----BEGIN PGP MESSAGE-----
Version: 2.6.2

hEwDfOTG8eEvuiEBAf9rxBdHpgdq1g0gaIP7zm1OcHvWHtx+9++ip27q6vI
tjYbIUKDnGjV0sm2INWpcohrarI9S2xU6UcSPyFfumGs9pgAAAQ0euRGjZY
RgIPE5DUHG uItXYsnIq7zFHVevjO2dAEJ8ouaIX9YJD8kwp4T3suQnw7/d
1j4edl46qisrQHpRRwqHXons7w4k04x8tH4JGfWEXc5LB+hcOSyPHEir4EP
qDcEPlblM9bH6 w2ku2fUmdMaoptnVSinLMtzSqIKQlHMfaJ0HM9Df4kWh+
ZbY0yFXxSuHKrgbaoDcu9wUze35dtwiCTdf1sf3ndQNaLOFiIjh5pis+bUg
9rOZjxpEFbdGgYpcfBB4rvRNwOwizvSodxJ9H+VdtAL3DIsSJdNSAEuxjQ0
hvOSA8oCBDJfHSUFqX3ROtB3+yuT1vf/C8Vod4gW4tvqj8C1QNte+ehxg==
=fD44
-----END PGP MESSAGE-----
```

Figure 2-8. Message after encryption

Signing

In addition, a public-key encryption system can be used to authenticate messages. In cases where the content of the message is not confidential, the receiver may still wish to verify the sender's identity. For example, one of your friends may find it amusing to have some fun at your expense (see Figure 2-9).

```
       To:     Rick Watson <rwatson@uga.edu>
     From:     President@whitehouse.gov
  Subject:     Invitation to visit the White House
------------------------------------------------------------
Dear Dr. Watson
It is my pleasure to invite you to a special meeting of Internet
users at the White House on April 1st at 2pm. Please call 212-123-
7890 and ask for Mr. A. Phool for complete details of your visit.

The President
```

Figure 2-9. Message before signing

If the President indeed were in the habit of communicating electronically, it is likely that he would sign his messages so that the receiver could verify it. A sender's private key is used to create a signed message. The receiver then applies the sender's public key to verify the signature (see Figure 2-10).

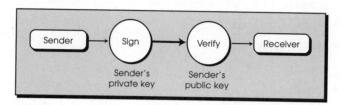

Figure 2-10. Signing with a public-key system

A signed message has additional encrypted text containing the sender's signature (see Figure 2-11). When the purported sender's public key is applied to this message, the identity of the sender can be verified (it was not the President).

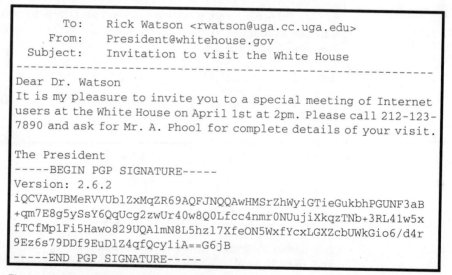

```
      To:     Rick Watson <rwatson@uga.cc.uga.edu>
    From:     President@whitehouse.gov
 Subject:     Invitation to visit the White House
------------------------------------------------------------
Dear Dr. Watson
It is my pleasure to invite you to a special meeting of Internet
users at the White House on April 1st at 2pm. Please call 212-123-
7890 and ask for Mr. A. Phool for complete details of your visit.

The President
-----BEGIN PGP SIGNATURE-----
Version: 2.6.2
iQCVAwUBMeRVVUblZxMqZR69AQFJNQQAwHMSrZhWyiGTieGukbhPGUNF3aB
+qm7E8g5ySsY6QqUcg2zwUr40w8Q0Lfcc4nmr0NUujiXkqzTNb+3RL41w5x
fTCfMp1Fi5Hawo829UQAlmN8L5hzl7XfeON5WxfYcxLGXZcbUWkGio6/d4r
9Ez6s79DDf9EuDlZ4qfQcy1iA==G6jB
-----END PGP SIGNATURE-----
```

Figure 2-11. Message after signing

Imagine you pay $1,000 (€910) per year for an investment information service. The provider might want to verify that any e-mail requests it receives are from subscribers. Thus, as part of the subscription sign-up, subscribers have to supply their public key, and when using the service, sign all electronic messages with their private key. The provider is then assured that it is servicing paying customers. Naturally, any messages between the service and the client should be encrypted to ensure that others do not gain from the information.

Electronic money

When commerce goes electronic, the means of paying for goods and services must also go electronic. Paper-based payment systems cannot support the speed, security, privacy, and internationalization necessary for electronic commerce. In this section, we discuss four methods of electronic payment:

- electronic funds transfer
- digital cash
- ecash
- credit card

There are four fundamental concerns regarding electronic money: security, authentication, anonymity, and divisibility. Consumers and organizations need to be assured that their on-line orders are protected, and organizations must be able to transfer securely many millions of dollars. Buyers and sellers must be able to verify that the electronic money they receive is real; consumers must have faith in electronic currency. Transactions, when required, should remain confidential. Electronic currency must be spendable in small amounts (e.g., less than one-tenth of a cent) so that high-volume, small-value Internet transactions are feasible (e.g., paying 0.1 cent to read an article in an encyclopedia). The various approaches to electronic money vary in their capability to solve these concerns (see Table 2-4).

Table 2-4: Characteristics of electronic money

	Security	Authentication	Anonymity	Divisibility
EFT	High	High	Low	Yes
Digital cash	Medium	High	High	Yes
Ecash	High	High	High	Yes
Credit card	High	High	Low	Yes

Any money system, real or electronic, must have a reasonable level of security and a high level of authentication, otherwise people will not use it. All electronic money systems are potentially divisible. There is a need, however, to adapt some systems so that transactions can be automated. For example, you do not want to have to type your full credit card details each time you spend one-tenth of a cent. A modified credit card system, which automatically sends previously stored details from your personal computer, could be used for small transactions.

The technical problems of electronic money have not been completely solved, but many people are working on their solution because electronic money promises efficiencies that will reduce the costs of transactions between buyers and sellers. It will also enable access to the global marketplace. In the next few years, electronic currency will displace notes and coins for many transactions.

Electronic funds transfer

Electronic funds transfer (EFT), introduced in the late 1960s, uses the existing banking structure to support a wide variety of payments. For example, consumers can establish monthly checking account deductions for utility bills, and banks can transfer millions of dollars. EFT is essentially electronic checking. Instead of writing a check and mailing it, the buyer initiates an electronic checking transaction (e.g., using a debit card at a point-of-sale terminal). The transaction is then electronically transmitted to an intermediary (usually the banking system), which transfers the funds from the buyer's account to the seller's account. A banking system has one or more common clearinghouses that facilitate the flow of funds between accounts in different banks.

Electronic checking is fast; transactions are instantaneous. Paper handling costs are substantially reduced. Bad checks are no longer a problem because the seller's account balance is verified at the moment of the transaction. EFT is flexible; it can handle high volumes of consumer and commercial transactions, both locally and internationally. The international payment clearing system, consisting of more than 100 financial institutions, handles more than one trillion dollars per day.

The major shortfall of EFT is that all transactions must pass through the banking system, which is legally required to record every transaction. This lack of privacy can have serious consequences.[2] Cash gives anonymity.

Digital cash

Digital cash is an electronic parallel of notes and coins. Two variants of digital cash are presently available: prepaid cards and smart cards. The phonecard, the most common form of prepaid card, was first issued in 1976 by the forerunner of Telecom Italia. The problem with special-purpose cards, such as phone and photocopy cards, is that people end up with a purse or wallet full of cards. A smart card combines many functions into one card. A smart card can serve as personal identification, credit card, ATM card, telephone credit card, critical

---

2. A defrocked Buddhist monk left a credit card transaction trail when he visited an Australian brothel (Police asked to examine credit card pay slips. *Bangkok Post.* Feb. 24 1995; 50(55):1).

medical information record and as *cash* for small transactions. A smart card, containing memory and a microprocessor, can store as much as 100 times more data than a magnetic-stripe card. The microprocessor can be programmed.

The stored-value card, the most common application of smart card technology, can be used to purchase a wide variety of items (e.g,. fast food, parking, public transport tickets). Consumers buy cards of standard denominations (e.g., $50 or €100) from a card dispenser or bank. When the card is used to pay for an item, it must be inserted in a reader. Then, the amount of the transaction is transferred to the reader, and the value of the card is reduced by the transaction amount.

The problem with digital cash, like real cash, is that you can lose it or it can be stolen. It is not as secure as the other alternatives, but most people are likely to carry only small amounts of digital cash and thus security is not so critical. As smart cards are likely to have a unique serial number, consumers can limit their loss by reporting a stolen or misplaced smart card to invalidate its use. Adding a PIN number to a smart card can raise its security level.

Twenty million smart cards are already in use in France, where they were introduced a decade earlier. In Austria, 2.5 million consumers carry a card that has an ATM magnetic stripe as well as a smart card chip. Stored-value cards are likely to be in widespread use in the United States within five years. Their wide-scale adoption could provide substantial benefits. Counting, moving, storing and safeguarding cash is estimated to be 4 percent of the value of all transactions. There are also significant benefits to be gained because banks don't have to hold as much cash on hand, and thus have more money available for investment.

Ecash

Digicash of Amsterdam has developed an electronic payment system called ecash that can be used to withdraw and deposit electronic cash over the Internet. The system is designed to provide secure payment between computers using e-mail or the Internet. Ecash can be used for everyday Internet transactions, such as buying software, receiving money from parents, or paying for a pizza to be delivered. At the same time, ecash provides the privacy of cash because the payer can remain anonymous.

To use ecash, you need a digital bank account and ecash client software. The client is used to withdraw ecash from your bank account, and store it on your personal computer. You can then spend the money at any location accepting ecash or send money to someone who has an ecash account.

The security system is based on public-key cryptography and passwords. You need a password to access your account and electronic transactions are encrypted.

Credit card

Credit cards are a safe, secure, and widely used remote payment system. Millions of people use them every day for ordering goods by phone. Furthermore, people think nothing of handing over their card to a restaurant server, who could easily find time to write down the card's details. In the case of fraud in the U.S., banks already protect consumers, who are typically liable for only the first $50 (€45). So, why worry about sending your credit card number over the Internet? The development of secure servers and clients has made transmitting credit card numbers extremely safe. The major shortcoming of credit cards is that they do not support person-to-person transfers and do not have the privacy of cash.

Secure electronic transactions

Electronic commerce requires participants to have a secure means of transmitting the confidential data necessary to perform a transaction. For instance, banks (which bear the brunt of the cost of credit card fraud) prefer credit card numbers to be hidden from prying electronic eyes. In addition, consumers want assurance that the Web site with which they are dealing is not a bogus operation. Two forms of protecting electronic transactions are SSL and SET.

SSL

Secure Sockets Layer (SSL) was created by Netscape for managing the security of message transmissions in a network. SSL uses public-key encryption to encode the transmission of secure messages (e.g., those containing a credit card number) between a browser and a Web server.

The client part of SSL is part of Netscape's browser. If a Web site is using a Netscape server, SSL can be enabled and specific Web pages can be identified as requiring SSL access. Other servers can be enabled by using Netscape's SSLRef program library, which can be downloaded for noncommercial use or licensed for commercial use.

SET

Secure Electronic Transaction (SET) is a financial industry innovation designed to increase consumer and merchant confidence in electronic commerce. Backed by major credit card companies, MasterCard and Visa, SET is designed to offer a high level of security for Web-based financial transactions. SET should reduce consumers' fears of purchasing over the Web and increase use of credit cards for electronic shopping. A proposed revision, due in 1999, will extend SET to support business-to-business transactions, such as inventory payments.

Euroding the European markets for American companies

Some analysts are warning that the introduction of the euro will help European companies develop their markets at the expense of U.S. companies hoping to penetrate the European e-commerce markets. Pricing all items in euros will allow Europeans to understand the value of items in other euro-based countries once they internalize the euro's relationship to their home currency, and especially when the individual currencies are phased out. Also, if as predicted, the euro weakens to a par value with the U.S. dollar (it's now worth about $1.10), even American prices will be easily understood.

The *euro zone* of 11 different countries is currently larger than the U.S. market and could be about 33 percent larger if the four other European countries not now participating in the currency ultimately adopt it.

Europeans might spend more on-line. The average per capita on-line expenditure in the Netherlands is $400 (€364), compared with $250 (€227) in the U.S. This may be explained by fewer retail hours per week in Europe than in the U.S.

Since its use is optional until 2002, the euro will not have much immediate impact on retail business-to-consumer e-commerce. However, over the next few years, Web retailers that have, or want, significant European business should start pricing their goods in euros even though this will mean repricing on a daily basis to allow for exchange rate fluctuations.

The introduction of the euro is already making life easier for businesses dealing within the euro zone, saving them from foreign exchange transaction costs and having to maintain accounts in different currencies. It will be easier to trade across borders, with a resultant larger market.

The euro will not solve all problems for American companies trying to enter the European markets. Different voltages, outlet plugs, telephone connectors, videotape formats, languages, cultures, taxation, and regulatory issues will still be around to cause complications.

American companies trying to enter the European market could look to forming partnerships with European companies. The gourmet food gift site GreatFood.com doesn't ship outside the United States because of customs restrictions on perishable food. To crack the international market, they need partners inside the euro zone as well as in Asia.

Adapted from Gardner, E. 1998. Euro seen as mixed blessing for U.S. e-commerce companies. *Internet World*, Feb. 8, 1, 41.

Visa and MasterCard founded SET as a joint venture on February 1, 1996. They realized that in order to promote electronic commerce, consumers and merchants would need a secure, reliable payment system. In addition, credit card issuers sought the protection of more advanced anti-fraud measures. American Express has subsequently joined the venture.

SET is based on cryptography and digital certificates. Public-key cryptography ensures message confidentiality between parties in a financial transaction. **Digital certificates** uniquely identify the parties to a transaction. They are issued by banks or clearinghouses and kept in registries so that authenticated users can look up other users' public keys.

Think of a digital certificate as an electronic credit card. It contains a person's name, a serial number, expiration date, a copy of the certificate holder's public key (used for encrypting and decrypting messages and verifying digital signatures), and the digital signature of the certificate-issuing authority so that a recipient can verify that the certificate is real. A **digital signature** is used to guarantee a message sender's identity.

The SET components

Cardholder wallet

The application on the cardholder's side is also called the *digital wallet*. This software plug-in contains a consumer's digital certificate, shipping and other account information. This critical information is protected by a password, which the owner must supply to access the stored data. In effect, an electronic wallet stores a digital representation of a person's credit card and enables electronic transactions.

Merchant server

On the merchant side, a merchant server accepts electronic credit card payments.

Payment gateway

The payment gateway is the bridge between SET and the existing payment network. A payment gateway application translates SET messages for the existing payment system to complete the electronic transaction.

Certificate authority

The certificate authority issues and manages digital certificates, which are proofs of the identities for all parties involved in a SET transaction.

The process

The following set of steps illustrates SET in action.

1. The customer opens a MasterCard or Visa account with a bank.

2. The customer receives a digital certificate (an electronic file), which functions as a credit card for on-line transactions. The certificate includes

a public key with an expiration date and has been digitally signed by the bank to ensure its validity.

3. Third-party merchants also receive digital certificates from the bank. These certificates include the merchant's public key and the bank's public key.

4. The customer places an electronic order from a merchant's Web page.

5. The customer's browser receives and confirms that the merchant's digital certificate is valid.

6. The browser sends the order information. This message is encrypted with the merchant's public key, the payment information, which is encrypted with the bank's public key (which can't be read by the merchant), and information that ensures the payment can be used only with the current order.

7. The merchant verifies the customer by checking the digital signature on the customer's certificate. This may be done by referring the certificate to the bank or to a third-party verifier.

8. The merchant sends the order message along to the bank. This includes the bank's public key, the customer's payment information (which the merchant can't decode), and the merchant's certificate.

9. The bank verifies the merchant and the message. The bank uses the digital signature on the certificate with the message and verifies the payment part of the message.

10. The bank digitally signs and sends authorization to the merchant, who can then fill the order.

11. The customer receives the goods and a receipt.

12. The merchant gets paid according to its contract with its bank.

13. The customer gets a monthly bill from the bank issuing the credit card.

The advantage of SET is that a consumer's credit card number cannot be deciphered by the merchant. Only the bank and card issuer can decode this number. This facility provides an additional level of security for consumers, banks, and credit card issuers, because it significantly reduces the ability of unscrupulous merchants to establish a successful Web presence.

In order to succeed, SET must displace the current standard for electronic transactions, SSL, which is simpler than SET but less secure. Because of SSL's simplicity, it is expected to provide tough competition, and may remain the method of choice for the interface between the on-line buyer and the merchant. The combination of SSL and fraud-detection software has so far provided low-cost, adequate protection for electronic commerce.

Cookies

The creator of a Web site often wants to remember facts about you and your visit. A **cookie** is the mechanism for remembering details of a single visit or store facts between visits. A cookie is a small file (not more than 4k) stored on your hard disk by a Web application. Cookies have several uses.

- **Visit tracking:** A cookie might be used to determine which pages a person views on a particular Web site visit. The data collected could be used to improve site design.

- **Storing information:** Cookies are used to record personal details so that you don't have to supply your name and address details each time you visit a particular site. Most subscription services (e.g., The Wall Street Journal) and on-line stores (e.g., Amazon.com) use this approach.

- **Customization:** Some sites use cookies to customize their service. A cookie might be used by CNN to remember that you are mainly interested in news about ice skating and cooking.

- **Marketing:** A cookie can be used to remember what sites you have visited so that relevant advertisements can be supplied. For example, if you frequently visit travel sites, you might get a banner ad from Delta popping up next time you do a search.

Cookies are a useful way of collecting data to provide visitors with better service. Without accurate information about people's interest, it is very difficult to provide good service.

Both Internet Explorer and Netscape Navigator allow surfers to set options for various levels of warnings about the use of cookies. Visitors who are concerned about the misuse of cookies can reject them totally, with the consequent loss of service.

Conclusion

The rapid growth of electronic commerce is clear evidence of the reliability and robustness of the underlying technology. Many of the pieces necessary to facilitate electronic commerce are mature, well-tested technologies, such as public-key encryption. The future is likely to see advances that make electronic commerce faster, less expensive, more reliable, and more secure.

Cases

Austin, R. D., and M. Cotteleer. 1997. *Ford Motor Company: maximizing the business value of Web technologies*. Harvard Business School, 9-198-006.

Parent, M. 1997. *Cisco Systems Inc.: managing corporate growth using an Intranet*. London, Canada: University of Western Ontario. 997E018.

References

Applegate, L. M., C. W. Holsapple, R. Kalakota, F. J. Rademacher, and A. B. Whinston. 1996. Electronic commerce: building blocks for new business opportunity. *Journal of Organizational Computing and Electronic Commerce* 6 (1):1-10.

Kalakota, R., and A. B. Whinston. 1996. *Frontiers of electronic commerce.* Reading, MA: Addison-Wesley.

Watson, R. T., P. G. McKeown, and M. Garfield. 1997. Topologies for electronic cooperation. In *Telekoopertion in Unternehmen*, edited by F. Lehner and S. Dustdar. Weisbaden, Germany: Deutscher Universitäts Verlag, 1-11.

3

Web strategy: Attracting and retaining visitors

Introduction

The Web changes the nature of communication between firms and customers. The traditional advertiser decides the message content, and on the Web, the customer selects the message. Traditional advertising primarily centers on the firm broadcasting a message. The flow of information is predominantly from the seller to the buyer. However, the Web puts this flow in reverse thrust. Customers have considerable control over which messages they receive because it is primarily by visiting Web sites that they are exposed to marketing communications. The customer intentionally seeks the message.[1]

The Web increases the richness of communication because it enables greater interactivity between the firm and its customers and among customers. The airline can e-mail frequent flyers special deals on underbooked flights. The prospective book buyer can search electronically by author, title, or genre. Customers can join discussion groups to exchange information on product bugs, innovative uses, gripes about service, and ask each other questions. Firms and customers can get much closer to each other because of the relative ease and low cost of electronic interaction.

Although there is some traditional advertising on the Web, especially that associated with search engines, in the main the communication relationship is distinctly different. This shift in communication patterns is so profound that major communication conglomerates are undergoing a strategic realignment. Increasingly, customers use search and directory facilities to seek information about a firm's products and services. Consequently, persuading and motivating customers to seek out interactive marketing communication and interact with advertisers is the biggest challenge facing advertisers in the interactive age.

In the new world of Web advertising, the rules are different. The Web, compared to other media, provides a relatively level playing field for all participants in that:

---

1. This chapter is based on Watson, R. T., S. Akselsen, and L. F. Pitt. 1998. Attractors: building mountains in the flat landscape of the World Wide Web. *California Management Review* 40 (2):36-56.

- access opportunities are essentially equal for all players, regardless of size;

- share of voice is essentially uniform—no player can drown out others;

- initial set-up costs present minimal or nonexistent barriers to entry.

A small company with a well-designed home page can look every bit as professional and credible as a large, multinational company. People can't tell if you do business from a 90-story office building or a two-room rented suite. Web home pages level the playing field for small companies.

Differentiation—success in appealing to desirable market segments so as to maintain visibility, create defensible market positions, and forge institutional identity—is considered to be a central key to survival and growth for businesses in the new electronic marketplace. In other words:

How do you create a mountain in a flat world?

An **attractor** is a Web site with the potential to attract and interact with a relatively large number of visitors in a target stakeholder group (for example, an auto company will want to attract and interact with more prospective buyers to its Web site than its competitors). While the Web site must be a good attractor, it must also have the facility for interaction if its powers of attraction are to have a long life span. Merely having attraction power is not enough—the site might attract visitors briefly or only once. The strength of the medium lies in its abilities to interact with buyers, on the first visit and thereafter. Good sites offer interaction above all else; less effective sites may often look more visually appealing, but offer little incentive to interact. Many organizations have simply used the Web as an electronic dumping ground for their corporate brochures—this in no way exploits the major attribute of the medium—its ability to interact with the visitor. Purely making the corporate Web site a mirror of the brochure is akin to a television program that merely presents visual material in the form of stills, with little or no sound. Television's major attribute is its ability to provide motion pictures and sounds to a mass audience, and merely using it as a platform for showing still graphics and pictures does not exploit the medium. Thus, very little television content is of this kind today. Similarly, if Web sites are not interactive, they fail to exploit the potential of the new medium. The best Web sites both attract and interact—for example, the BMW site shows pictures of its cars and accompanies these with textual information. More importantly, BMW allows the visitor to see and listen to the new BMW Z3 coupe, redesign the car by seeing different color schemes and specifications, and drive the car using virtual reality. This is interaction with the medium rather than mere reaction to the medium.

We propose that the strategic use of hard-to-imitate attractors, building blocks for gaining visibility with targeted stakeholders, will be a key factor in on-line marketing. Creating an attractor will, we believe, become a key component of the strategy of some firms. This insight helps define the issues we want to focus on in this chapter:

- identification and classification of attractors;
- use of attractors to support a marketing strategy.

Types of attractors

Given the recency of the Web, there is limited prior research on electronic commerce, and theories are just emerging. In new research domains, observation and classification are common features of initial endeavors. Thus, in line with the pattern coding approach of qualitative research, we sought overriding concepts to classify attractors.

To understand how firms distinguish themselves in a flat world, we reviewed marketing research literature, surfed many Web sites (including specific checks on innovations indicated in What's New pages or sections), monitored Web sites that publish reviews of other companies' Web efforts, and examined prize lists for innovative Web solutions.

After visiting many Web sites and identifying those that seem to have the potential to attract a large number of visitors, we used metaphors to label and group sites into categories (see Table 3-1). The categories are not mutually exclusive, just as the underlying metaphors are not distinct categories. For example, we use both the archive and entertainment park as metaphors. In real life, archives have added elements of entertainment (e.g., games that demonstrate scientific principles) and entertainment parks recreate historical periods (e.g., Frontierland at Disney).

Table 3-1: Types of attractors

The entertainment park
The archive
Exclusive sponsorship
The Town Hall
The club
The gift shop
The freeway intersection or portal
The customer service center

The entertainment park

Web sites in this category engage visitors in activities that demand a high degree of participation while offering entertainment. Many use games to market products and enhance corporate image. These sites have the potential to generate experiential flow, because they provide various degrees of challenge to visitors. They are interactive and often involve elements and environments that promote telepresence experiences. The activities in the entertainment park often have the character of a contest, where awards can be distributed through the network (e.g., the Disney site). These attractors are interactive, recreational, and challenging. The potential competitive advantages gained through these attractors are high traffic potential (with repeat visits) and creation or enforcement of an image of a dynamic, exciting, and friendly corporation.

Examples in this category include:

- GTE Laboratories' *Fun Stuff* part of its Web site, which includes Web versions of the popular games MineSweeper, Rubik's cube, and a 3D maze for Web surfers to navigate;

- The Kellogg Company's site lets young visitors pick a drawing and color it by selecting from a palette and clicking on segments of the picture;

- Visitors to Karakas VanSickle Ouellette Advertising and Public Relations can engage in the comical *Where's Pierre* game and win a T-shirt by discovering the whereabouts of Pierre Ouellette, *KVO's creative big cheese*;

- Joe Boxer uses unusual effects and contests for gaining attention. For solving an advanced puzzle, winners gain supplies of virtual underwear. Instructions such as "Press the eyeball and you will return to the baby," are a blend of insanity and advertising genius.

The archive

Archive sites provide their visitors with opportunities to discover the historical aspects of the company's activities. Their appeal lies in the instant and universal access to interesting information and the visitor's ability to explore the past, much like museums or maybe even more like the more recently created exploratoria (entertainment with educational elements). The credibility of a well-established image is usually the foundation of a successful archive, and building and reinforcing this corporate image is the main marketing role of the archive.

The strength of these attractors is that they are difficult to imitate, and often impossible to replicate. They draw on an already established highly credible feature of the company, and they bring an educational potential, thus reinforcing public relations aspects of serving the community with valuable information. The major weakness is that they often lack interactivity and are static and less likely to attract repeat visits. The potential competitive advantage gained through these attractors is the building and maintenance of the image of a trusted, reputable, and well-established corporation.

Examples in this category include:

- Ford's historical library of rare photos and a comprehensive story of the Ford Motor Company;

- Boeing's appeal to aircraft enthusiasts by giving visitors a chance to find out more about its aircraft through pictures, short articles on new features, and technical explanations;

- Hewlett-Packard's site where everyone can check out the Palo Alto garage in which Bill Hewlett and Dave Packard started the firm.

Exclusive sponsorship

An organization may be the exclusive sponsor of an event of public interest, and use its Web site to extend its audience reach. Thus, we find on the Internet details of sponsored sporting competitions and broadcasts of special events such as concerts, speeches, and the opening of art exhibitions.

Sponsorship attractors have broad traffic potential and can attract many visitors in short periods (e.g., the World Cup). They can enhance the image of the corporation through the provision of timely, exclusive, and valuable information. However, the benefits of the Web site are lost unless the potential audience learns of its existence. This is a particular problem for short-term events when there is limited time to create customer awareness. Furthermore, the information on the Web site must be current. Failure to provide up-to-the-minute results for many sporting events could have an adverse effect on the perception of an organization.

Examples of sponsorship include:

- Texaco publishes the radio schedule for the Metropolitan Opera, which it sponsors on National Public Radio;

- Coca-Cola gives details of Coke-sponsored concerts and sporting events;

- Planet Reebok includes interviews with the athletes it sponsors. The Web site permits visitors to post questions to coaches and players.

A Web site can provide a venue for advertisers excluded from other media. For instance, cigarette manufacturer Rothmans, the sponsor of the Cape Town to Rio de Janeiro yacht race, has a Web site devoted to this sporting event.

The town hall

The traditional town hall has long been a venue for assembly where people can hear a famous person speak, attend a conference, or participate in a seminar. The town hall has gone virtual, and these public forums are found on the Web.

These attractors can have broad traffic potential when the figure is of national importance or is a renowned specialist in a particular domain. Town halls have a potentially higher level of interactivity and participation and can be more engaging than sponsorship. However, there is the continuing problem of advising the potential audience of who is appearing. There is a need for a parallel bulletin board to notify interested attendees about the details of town hall events. Another problem is to find a continual string of drawing card guests.

Examples in this category are:

- Tripod, a resource center for college students, has daily interviews with people from a wide variety of areas. Past interviews are archived under categories of Living, Travel, Work, Health, Community, and Money.

- CMP Publications Inc., a publisher of IT magazines (e.g., *InformationWeek*), hosts a Cyberforum, where an IT guru posts statements on a topic (e.g., Windows 2000) and responds to issues raised by readers.

The club

People have a need to be part of a group and have satisfactory relationships with others. For some people, a Web club can satisfy this need. These are places to *hang out* with your friends or those with similar interests. On the Internet, the club is an electronic community, which has been a central feature of the Internet since its foundation. Typically, visitors have to register or become members to participate, and they often adopt electronic personas when they enter the club. Web clubs engage people because they are interactive and recreational. Potentially, these attractors can increase company loyalty, enhance customer feedback, and improve customer service through *members helping members*.

Examples include:

- Snapple Beverage Company gives visitors the opportunity to meet each other with personal ads (free) that match people using attributes such as favorite Snapple flavor;

- Zima's loyalty club, Tribe Z, where members can access exclusive areas of the site;

- Apple's EvangeList, a bulletin board for maintaining the faith of Macintosh devotees.

An interesting extension of this attractor is the electronic trade show, with attached on-line chat facilities in the form of a MUD (multiuser dungeon) or MOO (multiuser dungeon object oriented). Here visitors can take on roles and exchange opinions about products offered at the show.

48

The gift shop

Gifts and free samples nearly always get attention. Web gifts typically include digitized material such as software (e.g., screensavers and utilities), photographs, digital paintings, research reports, and non-digital offerings (e.g., a T-shirt). Often, gifts are provided as an explicit bargain for dialogue participation (e.g., the collection of demographic data).

Examples include:

- Ameritech's Claude Monet exhibition where you can download digital paintings;

- Kodak's library of colorful, high-quality digital images that are downloadable;

- Ragu Foods offers recipes, Italian-language lessons, merchandise, and stories written by Internet users. You can e-mail a request for product coupons. There is culture, too, in the form of an architectural tour of a typical Pompeiian house;

- MCA/Universal Cyberwalk offers audio and video clips from upcoming Universal Pictures' releases, and a virtual tour of Universal Studios, Hollywood's new ride based on *Back to the Future*. There is even a downloadable coupon hidden in the area that will let you bypass the line for the ride at the theme park.

One noteworthy subspecies of the gift is the software utility or update. Many software companies distribute upgrades and complimentary freeware or shareware via their Web site. In some situations (e.g., a free operating system upgrade), this can generate overwhelming traffic for one or two weeks. Because some software vendors automatically notify registered customers by e-mail whenever they add an update or utility, such sites can have bursts of excessively high attractiveness.

The freeway intersections or portals

Web sites that provide advanced information processing services (e.g., search engines) can become n-dimensional Web freeway intersections with surfers coming and going in all directions, and present significant advertising opportunities because the traffic flow is intense—rather like traditional billboard advertising in Times Square or Picadilly Circus. Search engines, directories, news centers, and electronic malls can attract hundreds of thousands of visitors in a day.

Some of these sites are entry points to the Web for many people, and are known as portals. These portals are massive on-ramps to the Internet. A highly successful portal, such as America Online, attracts a lot of traffic.

Within this category, we also find sites that focus upon specific customer segments and try to become their entry points to the Web. Demography (e.g., an interest in fishing) and geography (such as Finland Online's provision of an extensive directory for Finland) are possible approaches to segmentation. The goal is to create a one-stop resource center. First movers who do the job well are likely to gain a long-term competitive advantage because they have secured prime real estate, or what conventional retailers might call a virtual location.

Examples include:

- Yahoo!, a hierarchical directory of Web sites;
- ISWorld, an entry point to serve the needs of information systems academics and students;
- AltaVista, a Web search engine originally operated by Digital (since acquired by Compaq Computers) as a means of promoting its Alpha servers.

The customer service center

By directly meeting their information needs, a Web site can be highly attractive to existing customers. Many organizations now use their Web site to support the ownership phase of the customer service life cycle. For instance, Sprint permits customers to check account balances, UPS has a parcel tracking service, many software companies support downloading of software updates and utilities (e.g., Adobe), and many provide answers to FAQs or frequently asked questions (e.g., Fuji Film). The Web site is a customer service center. When providing service to existing customers, the organization also has the opportunity to sell other products and services. A visitor to the Apple Web site, for example, may see the special of the week displayed prominently.

Leading the charge after deregulation

With deregulation allowing consumers to choose their energy providers, oil and gas companies have to adopt measures to attract customers. One company is already investing millions of dollars to take advantage of the free market. Columbia Energy Inc. is creating a network of 100 local and regional Web sites where potential customers can sign up on-line. These sites offer services such as on-line bill payment, tools for at-home energy audits, and assistance with buying appliances. Within the first month, these sites generated 4 percent of the company's new customers in Georgia.

While giving its customers better service, Columbia Energy Inc. can reduce the costs associated with monthly mailings and service calls.

Adapted from Machlis, S. 1998. Utility powers up Net strategy to lure customers. *Computerworld*, Dec. 7, 4.

Summary

Organizations are taking a variety of approaches to making their Web sites attractive to a range of stakeholders. Web sites can attract a broad audience, some of whom are never likely to purchase the company's wares, but could influence perceptions of the company, and certainly increase word-of-mouth communication, which could filter through to significant real customers. Other Web sites focus on serving one particular stakeholder—the customer. They can aim to increase market share by stimulating traffic to their site (e.g., Kellogg's) or to increase the share of the customer by providing superior service (e.g., the UPS parcel tracking service).

Of course, an organization is not restricted to using one form of attractor. It makes good sense to take a variety of approaches so as to maximize the attractiveness of a site and to meet the diverse needs of Web surfers. For example, Tripod uses a variety of attractors to draw traffic to its site. By making the site a drawing card for college students, Tripod can charge advertisers higher rates. As Table 3-2 illustrates, there are some gaps. Tripod is not an archive or the exclusive sponsor of an event.

Table 3-2: Tripod's use of attractors

Type of attractor	Tripod's approach
Entertainment park	Limited development, except for a novel concentration game, members can test their memory by matching different types of contraceptives.
Town Hall	Daily interviews on topics of likely interest to college students. Past interviews can be recalled.
Club	Only members can use *HereMOO*, a graphical, interactive environment in which members can interact. Visitors can join Tripod by providing some basic demographic data. Also, members can build a home page.
Gift shop	Every 25th new member wins a T-shirt and every 10th new member wins a bottle opener key chain. There are also weekly competitions.
Freeway intersection or portal	An entry point for a number of news services (e.g., *USA Today*) and stock prices provided by other Web sites.
Customer service center	A travel planner and daily reminder are examples of services that members can use.

Attractiveness factors

The previous examples illustrate the variety of tactics used by organizations to make their sites attractors. There is, however, no way of ensuring that we have identified a unique set of categories. There may be other types of attractors that we simply did not recognize or uncover in our search. To gain a deeper understanding of attractiveness, we examine possible dimensions for describing the relationship between a visitor and a Web site. The service design literature, and in particular the service process matrix, provide the stimulus for defining the elements of attractiveness.

The service process matrix (see Figure 3-1), with dimensions of degree of labor intensity and interaction and customization, identifies four types of service businesses. Labor-intensive businesses have a high ratio of cost of labor relative to the value of plant and equipment (e.g., law firms). A trucking firm, with a high investment in trucks, trailers, and terminals, has low labor intensity. Interaction and customization are, respectively, the extent to which the consumer interacts with the service process and the service is customized for the consumer.

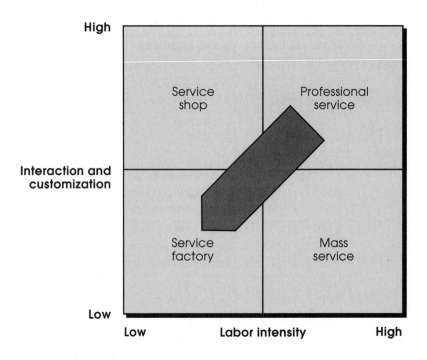

Figure 3-1. The service process matrix (Adapted from Schmenner)

Because services are frequently simultaneously produced and consumed, they are generally easier to customize than products. A soft drink manufacturer would find it almost impossible to mix a drink for each individual customer, while dentists tend to customize most of the time, by treating each patient as an individual. The question facing most firms, of course, is to what extent they wish to customize offerings.

For many services, customization and interaction are associated. High customization often means high interaction (e.g., an advertising agency) and low customization is frequently found with low interaction (e.g., fast food), though this is not always the case (e.g., business travel agents have considerable interaction with their customers but little customization because airline schedules are set). The push for lower costs and control is tending to drive services towards the diagonal. The traditional carrier, for example, becomes a no-frills airline by moving towards the lower-left.

If we now turn to the Web, labor intensity disappears as a key element because the Web is an automated service delivery system. Hence, we focus our attention on interaction and customization and split these out as two separate elements to create the attractors grid (see Figure 3-2). Attractors require varying degrees of visitor interaction. A search engine simply requires the visitor to enter search terms. While the customers may make many searches, on any one visit there is little interaction. Just like a real entertainment park, a Web park is entertaining only if the visitor is willing to participate (e.g., play an interactive game). The degree of customization varies across attractors from low (e.g., the digital archive) to high (e.g., a customer service center).

Each of the four quadrants in the attractors grid has a label. A utility (e.g., search engine) requires little interaction and there is no customization, each customer receives the same output for identical keywords. A service center provides information tailored to the customer's current concern (e.g., what is the balance of my account?). In mass entertainment (e.g., an entertainment park), the visitor participates in an enjoyable interaction, but there is no attempt to customize according to the needs or characteristics of the visitor. The atmosphere of a club is customized interaction. The club member feels at home because of the personalized nature of the interaction.

Our use of the terms utility and service center correspond closely to the categories of service factory and service shop in Figure 3-1. This similarity is not surprising since low labor-intensity tasks are often automated and performed by the customer (e.g., order taking). The high labor-intensity quadrants of the service process matrix (mass service and professional service) can potentially become Web applications if some or all of the provided service are delivered electronically. For instance, the law firm, a professional service, can reduce labor intensity by providing Web on-line services for clients and by providing a mass service.

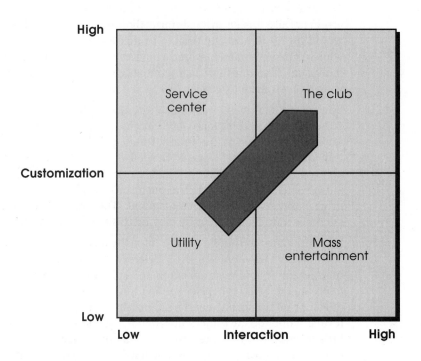

Figure 3-2. Attractors grid

In contrast to the service process matrix's push down the diagonal, the impetus with attractors should be towards customized service—up the diagonal (see Figure 3-2). The search engine, which falls in the utility quadrant, needs to discover more about its visitors so that it can become a customer service center. Similarly, mass entertainment should be converted to the personalized performance and interaction of a club. The service center can also consider becoming a club so that frequent visitors receive a special welcome and additional service, like hotel guests who are recognized by the concierge. Indeed, commercial Internet success may be dependent on creating clubs or electronic communities.

Where possible, organizations should be using the Web to reverse the trend away from customized service by creating highly customized attractors. Simultaneously, we could see the synergistic effects of both trends. A Web application reduces labor intensity and increases customization. This can come about because the model in Figure 3-1 assumes that people deliver services, but when services are delivered electronically, the dynamics change. In this respect, the introduction of the Web is a discontinuity for some service organizations, and represents an opportunity for some firms to change the structure of the industry.

A potential of the Web is that it will make mass customization work. It will enable customized service to each customer, while serving millions of them at the same time. All customers will get more or less what they want, tailored to what is unique to them and their circumstances. This will be achieved, almost without exception, by information technology. The really important aspect of this is that by mass customization, the firm will learn from customers; more importantly, customers are more likely to remain loyal, not so much because the firm serves them so well, but because they do not want to teach another firm what's already known about them by their current provider.

Sustainable attractiveness

The problem with many Web sites, like many good ideas, is that they are easily imitated. In fact, because the Web is so public, firms can systematically analyze each other's Web sites. They can continually monitor the Web presence of competitors and, where possible, quickly imitate many initiatives. Consequently, organizations need to be concerned with sustainable attractiveness—the ability to create and maintain a site that continues to attract targeted stakeholders. In the case of a Web site, sustainable attractiveness is closely linked to the ease with which a site can be imitated.

Attractors can be classified by ease of imitation, an assessment of the cost and time to copy another Web site's concept (see Table 3-3). The easiest thing to reproduce is information that is already in print (e.g., the corporate brochure). Product descriptions, annual reports, price lists, product photographs, and so forth can be converted quickly to HTML, GIFs, or an electronic publishing format such as Adobe's portable document format (PDF). Indeed, this sort of information is extremely common on the Web, and so bland that we consider it has minimal attractiveness.

Table 3-3: Ease of imitation of attractors

Ease of imitation	Examples of attractors
Easy	Corporate brochure
Imitate with some effort	Software utilities Directory or search engine
Costly to imitate	Advanced customer service application Sponsorship Valuable and rare resources
Impossible to imitate	Archive with some exclusive features Well-established brand name or corporate image

There is a variety of attractors, such as utilities, that can be imitated with some effort and time. The availability of multiple search engines and directories clearly supports this contention. The original offerer may gain from being a first mover, but distinctiveness will be hard to sustain. Nevertheless, while investing in easily imitated attractors may provide little gain, firms may have to match their competitors' offerings so as to remain equally attractive, thus echoing the notion of strategic necessity of the strategic information systems literature. Attractors are more like services than products. Innovations generally are more easily imitated, just as the first life insurance company to offer premium discounts to nonsmokers was easily imitated (and therefore not remembered).

While a search engine or directory can be imitated, what is less difficult to copy is location or identity. Some search engines are better placed than others. For example, clicking on Netscape's *Search* button gives immediate access to Netscape's search engine, and additional clicks are required to access competitive search engines. This is like being the first gas station after the freeway exit or the only one on a section of highway with long distances between exit ramps. It is one of the best pieces of real estate on the information superhighway, and certainly Netscape should gain a high rent for this spot.

The key to imitation is whether a firm possesses valuable and rare resources and how much it costs to duplicate these resources or how readily substitutes can be found. Back-end computer applications that support Web front-end customer service can be a valuable resource, though not rare. FedEx's parcel tracking service is an excellent example of a large investment back-end IT application easily imitated by competitor UPS. IT investment can create a competitive advantage, but it is unlikely to be sustainable because competitors can eventually duplicate the system.

Sponsorship is another investment that can create a difficult-to-imitate attractor. Signing a long-term contract to sponsor a major sporting or cultural event can create the circumstances for a long-lived attractor. Sponsorship is a rare resource, but its very rareness may induce competitors to escalate the cost of maintaining sponsorship for popular events. Contracts eventually run their course, and failure to win the next round of the bidding war will mean loss of the attractor.

There are some attractors that can never be imitated or for which there are few substitutes. No other beverage company can have a Coke Museum—real or virtual. Firms with respected and well-known brands (e.g., Coca-Cola) have a degree of exclusiveness that they can impart to their Web sites. The organization that owns a famous Monet painting can retain exclusive rights to offer the painting as a screensaver. For many people, there is no substitute for the Monet painting. These attractors derive their rareness from the reputation and history of the firm or the object. History can be a source of enduring competitiveness and, in this case, enduring attractiveness.

This analysis suggests that Web application designers should try to take advantage of:

- prior back-end IT investments that take time to duplicate;
- special relations (e.g., sponsorship);
- special information resources (e.g., an archive);
- established brand or image (part of the enterprise's history);
- proprietary intellectual/artistic capital (e.g., a Monet painting).

Strategies for attractors

Stakeholder analysis can be a useful tool for determining which types and forms of attractors to develop. Adapting the notion that a firm should sell to the most favorable buyers, an organization should concentrate on using its Web site to attract the most influential stakeholders. For example, it might use an attractor to communicate with employees or it may want to attract and inform investors and potential suppliers.

After selecting the targeted stakeholder group, the organization needs to decide the degree of focus of its attraction. We proffer a two-stage process for selecting the properties of an attractor (see Figure 3-3). First, identify the target stakeholder groups and make the site more attractive to these groups—the influence filter. Second, decide the degree of customization—the target refractor. For example, Kellogg's Web site, designed to appeal to all young children, filters but is not customized. American Airlines' Web site is an implementation of filtering and customization. The site is designed to attract prospective flyers (filtering). Frequent flyers, an important stakeholder group, have access to their mileage numbers by entering their frequent flyer number and a personal code (customization).

Broad attraction

A broad attractor can be useful for communicating with a number of types of stakeholders or many of the people in one category of stakeholders. Many archives, entertainment parks, and search engines have a general appeal, and there is no attempt to attract a particular segment of a stakeholder group. For example, Goodyear Tire & Rubber Company's Web site, with its information on tires, is directed at the general tire customer. A broad attractor provides content with minimal adjustment to the needs of the visitor. Thus, many visitors may not linger too long at the site because there is nothing that particularly catches their attention or meets a need. In terms of Figure 3-2, broad attractors are utilities or mass entertainment.

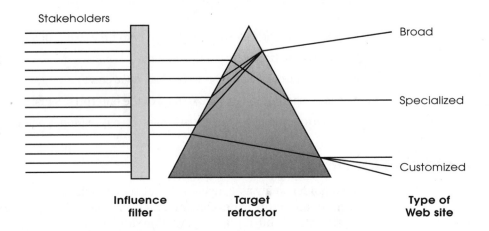

Stakeholders

Broad

Specialized

Customized

**Influence
filter**

**Target
refractor**

**Type of
Web site**

Figure 3-3. Attractor strategies

Specialized attraction

A specialized attractor appeals to a more narrow audience. UPS, with its parcel tracking system, has decided to focus on current customers. A customer can enter an tracking number to determine the current location of a package and download software for preparing transportation documentation. A specialized attractor can be situation dependent. It may attract fewer visitors, but nearly all those who make the link find the visit worthwhile. A specialized attractor may be a utility (providing solutions to a particular class of problem) or a service center (providing service to a specific group of stakeholders) (see Figure 3-2).

Personalized attractor

The marketer's goal is to develop an interactive relationship with individual customers. Personalized attractors, an incarnation of that dream, can be customized to meet the needs of the individual visitor. Computer magazine publisher Ziff-Davis offers visitors the opportunity to specify a personal profile. After completing a registration form, the visitor can then select what to see on future visits. For instance, a marketing manager tracking the CAD/CAM software market in Germany can set a profile that displays links to new stories on these topics. On future visits to the Ziff-Davis site, the manager can click on the personal view button to access the latest news matching the profile. The Mayo Clinic uses the Internet Chat facility to host a series of monthly on-line forums with Clinic specialists. The forums are free, and visitors may directly question an endocrinologist, for instance. Thus, visitors can get advice on their particular ailments.

There are two types of personalized attractors. **Adaptable** attractors can be customized by the visitor, as in the case of Ziff-Davis. The visitor establishes what is of interest by answering questions or selecting options. **Adaptive** attractors learn from the visitor's behavior and determine what should be presented. Advanced Web applications will increasingly use a visitor's previously gathered demographic data and record of pages browsed to create dynamically a personalized set of Web pages, just as magazines can be personalized.

One advantage of a personalized attractor is that it can create switching costs, which are not necessarily monetary, for the visitor. Although establishing a personal profile for an adaptable site is not a relatively high cost for the visitor, it can create some impediment to switching. An adaptive Web site further raises costs because the switching visitor will possibly have to suffer an inferior service while the new site learns what is relevant to the customer. Furthermore, an organization that offers an adaptable or adaptive Web site as a means of differentiation learns more about each customer. Since the capacity to differentiate is dependent on knowing the customer, the organization is better placed to further differentiate itself. Personalized attractors can provide a double payback—higher switching cost for customers and greater knowledge of each customer.

The flexibility of information technology means that organizations can build a Web page delivery platform that will produce a variety of customized pages. Thus, it is quite feasible for the visitor to determine before each access whether to receive a standard or customized page. For example, visitors could decide to receive the standard version of an electronic newspaper or one that they tailored. This choice might go hand in hand with a differential pricing mechanism so that visitors pay for customization, just as they do with many physical products. Flexible Web server systems should make it possible for organizations to provide simultaneously both broad and customized attractors. The choice then is not between types of attractors, but how much should the visitor pay for degrees of customization.

Conclusion

Because we often learn by modeling the behavior of others, we have used metaphors and examples to illustrate the variety of attractors that are currently operational. These should provide a useful starting point for practitioners designing attractors because a variety of stimuli are the most important means of stimulating creative behavior. However, we have no way of verifying that we have covered the range of metaphors, and other useful ones may emerge as organizations discover innovative uses of the Web. The attractors grid (see Figure 3-2) is a more formal method of classifying attractors, and provided we have identified the key parameters for describing attractors, does indicate complete coverage of the types of attractors.

Providing the personal touch to your portfolio

Providing close personal attention to each investor has been an important focus for Scudder Kemper Investments Inc. Its Web site uses artificial intelligence techniques, such as rules-based messaging and natural language interpretation, to provide a personalized on-line service.

The technology, supplied by Art Technology Group ATG, is based on its Dynamo application server and is designed to observe the behavior of visitors to the site and match these with a set of rules so as to personalize the service even before the visitor agrees to register.

The natural language processing is a search interface called the Financial Concierge, which interprets queries and provides the necessary feedback. The queries also feed into the Dynamo system looking for patterns to match interests.

Visitors can also create an on-line portfolio of their investments, including investments purchased from other firms. The site tracks the performance and issues any necessary warnings. There is no need for visitors to register until they have customized the site or created a portfolio and want to save preferences for another visit.

In addition to the increased personalization, Scudder is also making freely available content and services that are normally available only to registered users.

Adapted from Carr, D. F. 1999. How one investment site makes users feel special. *Internet World*, Feb. 8, 17-18.

The difference in the direction of the diagonal in the service process matrix and attractors grid suggests a discontinuity in the approach to delivering service. For some services, there should no longer be a reduction but an increase in customization as human-delivered services are replaced by Web service systems. Thus, this chapter provides two decision aids, metaphors and the attractor grid, for those attempting to identify potential attractors, and these challenge managers to rethink the current trend in service delivery.

The attractor strategy model is the third decision aid proffered. Its purpose is to stimulate thinking about the audience to be attracted and the degree of interactivity with it. The attractor strategy model is promoted as a tool for linking attractors to a stakeholder-driven view of strategy. In our view, attractors are strategic information systems and must be aligned with organizational goals.

Web sites have the potential for creating competitive advantage by attracting numerous visitors so that many potential customers learn about a firm's products and services or influential stakeholders gain a positive impression of the firm. The advantage, however, may be short-lived unless the organization has some valuable and rare resource (e.g., sponsorship of a popular sporting event) that cannot be duplicated. A valuable, but not necessarily rare, resource for many organizations is the current IT infrastructure. Firms should find it useful to re-examine their existing databases to gauge their potential for highly attractive Web applications. Building front-end Web applications to create an attractor (e.g., customer service) can be a quick way of capitalizing on existing investments, but competitors are likely to be undertaking the same projects. IT infrastructure, however, is not enough to create a sustained attractor. The key assets are managerial IT skills and viewing information as the key asset that can create competitive advantage. Sustainable attractiveness is dependent on managers understanding what information to deliver and how to present it to stakeholders.

Cases

Sviokla, J. 1996. Edmund's—www.edmunds.com. Harvard Business School, 9-397-016.

References

Armstrong, A., and J. Hagel. 1996. The real value of on-line communities. *Harvard Business Review* 74 (3):134-141.

Peppers, D., and M. Rogers. 1993. *The one to one future: building relationships one customer at a time.* New York, NY: Currency Doubleday.

Pine, B. J., B. Victor, and A. C. Boynton. 1993. Making mass customization work. *Harvard Business Review* 71 (5):108-119.

Schmenner, R. W. 1986. How can a service business prosper? *Sloan Management Review* 27 (3):21-32.

4

Promotion: Integrated Web communications

Introduction

Communication is the very heart of marketing, and for years companies have fashioned communication strategies based on print, radio, and TV media to broadcast their message, but times are changing. In the age of the Internet, Benetton uses Quicktime VR to establish the atmosphere of its retail outlets, ABN Amro has a banner advertisement directly behind the goal at an Internet soccer game; Sony provides downloadable audio clips of its latest CDs; and Voice of America makes available, via FTP, software for predicting high-frequency broadcast propagation. These companies recognize that the Internet is an all-purpose communication medium for interacting with a wide variety of stakeholders. They know they must manage their brands and corporate image in cyberspace. They also know that the Internet is not just the Web, but a range of technologies that, in combination, can be a potent marketing strategy.

As organizations stampede to the Internet, they need a systematic way to examine opportunities and relate them to available Internet tools. In particular, they need a cohesive marketing strategy for exploiting Internet technologies. Integrated Internet Marketing (I^2M) is a structured approach to combining marketing strategy with Internet technology. I^2M promotes creation of a strategy that synergistically exploits the range of Internet technologies (e.g., text, audio, video, and hyperlinking) to achieve marketing goals.

This chapter, abundantly illustrated with instances of how companies are using the Internet to market wisely, presents the I^2M model. A concluding case study demonstrates how one company, Benetton, is fashioning a coherent Internet-based strategy.

Internet technology for supporting marketing

To understand the potential of Internet marketing, knowledge of the different Internet tools is necessary. For convenience, some of these tools are grouped together and treated collectively because of common features (see Table 4-1).

Table 4-1: Internet technologies

Technology	Description	Examples
Asynchronous text	**E-mail** is generally used for one-to-one and one-to-few communications. A **bulletin board** (in the form of a newsgroup or listserv) can handle one-to-many and many-to-many communications.	Cathay Pacific uses a one-to-many bulletin board to advise prospective customers of special airfares. Claris uses bulletin boards in the many-to-many mode to support the exchange of ideas among customers and support staff.
Synchronous text	Chat enables several people to participate in a real-time text-based discussion. A chat session is conducted on a channel, and those connected to the channel receive all messages broadcast.	The American Booksellers Association uses chat to interview authors.
File transfer	File transfer protocol (FTP) permits the exchange of files across the Internet.	Oracle uses FTP to distribute a 90-day trial version of Power Objects, a software product.
Telnet	Telnet enables an authorized user to connect to and run programs on another computer.	The Library of Congress Information System (LOCIS) is accessible using Telnet.
Audio	Audio files are either downloaded and then played, or played as downloaded (so-called streaming audio).	ABC uses Progressive Network's RealAudio to deliver a news bulletin.
Video	Video files, like audio, are either downloaded and then played, or played as they are downloaded (so-called streaming video).	PBS uses VDOnet Corp. technology to broadcast samples of its programs.
Newswire	An electronic newswire broadcasts stock prices, sports scores, news, weather, and other items.	Companies are using Pointcast for reaching employees with internal news.
Search engine	A search engine supports finding information on the Web. Simple engines find Web pages. More advanced engines locate information based on defined attributes (e.g., cheapest model Y of brand X camera).	Internet Air Fares allows visitors the ability to search for the cheapest airfares on a particular route that they wish to travel.
Virtual reality	The visitor can look around a location through a full 360 degrees, as well as zoom in and out.	Honda use QuickTime VR to enable prospective customers to view its latest models, both inside and outside.

The Web as an integrating technology

The Web is the umbrella technology that can provide a single interface to each of the technologies previously described in Table 4-1. The hypertext feature of the Web enables links to be created within a document or to another document anywhere on the Web. This supports rapid navigation of Web sites. The multimedia capability means that a Web page can display graphics, and videos and play sound and animations, as well as provide support for on-line forms and multiple windows. The Web is the means by which a company can use a variety of Internet tools to interact with customers and other influential stakeholders. It can shape and direct the dialogue between an organization and its stakeholders. To a large extent, an organization's Web site defines the organization—establishing an enduring image in the minds of stakeholders. We maintain that organizations need a cohesive approach for using Internet technologies for communication.

What's "In Store" for the Web?

Retailers are now investigating ways of using the Web inside their stores. Recreational Equipment Inc. (REI), an outdoor equipment retailer, is testing sales terminals equipped with Web browsers in its stores.

These terminals allow the store assistant to access product and company information to place orders via the Web. Now the assistants can sell items that are out of stock in their store. Having access to customer information provides an opportunity to give a more personal service to the customer. Customers also have the option of placing their orders using kiosks located throughout the stores.

Other companies experimenting with in-store Web access include Gap Inc., while Burlington Coat Factory Warehouse Corp. is planning to provide its stores with access to the company's intranet.

Adapted from Orenstein, D. 1999. Retailers find uses for Web inside stores. *Computerworld*, Jan. 11, 41.

Integrated Internet Marketing

The interactive and multimedia capabilities of the Web, combined with other Internet facilities such as e-mail's support for personal and mass communication, present a range of tools for interacting with customers. Furthermore, the Web can provide an interface to back-end applications (e.g., databases and expert systems technology). Consequently, the Internet offers an excellent basis for a variety of marketing tactics, which permits the development of a model for Integrated Internet Marketing (I²M). The concepts of integrated Internet communication apply to all forms of communication, not just that between seller and buyer.

I²M (see Figure 4-1) is the coordination of Internet facilities to market products and services, shape stakeholders' (customers, in particular) attitudes, and establish or maintain a corporate image. The central idea of I²M is that an organization should coordinate its use of the Internet to develop a coherent, synchronous marketing strategy.

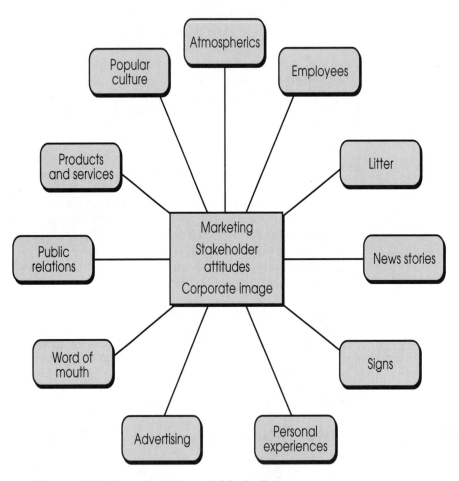

Figure 4-1. Integrated Internet Marketing

The Web offers a unique way to shape corporate image because it provides a means of communicating with so many stakeholder groups. For example, most organizations are interested in the ambiance or atmospherics that their establishment creates for the customer, where the term atmospherics refers to an organization's retail environment. The Web provides an opportunity for customers to experience an organization's atmospherics without actually being there (as the case later in this chapter demonstrates).

In the same way, the Web provides new opportunities in terms of signs, word of mouth, personal experiences, and public relations. Traditional marketing theory and practice have discovered that it is very difficult to manage a corporate image so that the identical image is communicated to every stakeholder group. The Web provides a powerful tool to assist managers in communicating a unified image.

The I²M matrix

The I²M matrix (see Table 4-2) can be used by firms to search systematically for opportunities for using the Internet to support marketing strategies. The concept is that each cell of the matrix is a focal point for brainstorming. An interactive version of the matrix,[1] on the Web of course, can be used to stimulate thinking by showcasing how organizations are using a particular cell. Thus, clicking on the cell at the intersection of Atmospherics and Asynchronous text would jump to a page containing links to organizations using asynchronous text (e.g., a bulletin board) to establish atmosphere. Apple, an example for this cell, has established a bulletin board, EvangeList, to keep the faith of Macintosh aficionados. Postings to this bulletin board evoke an image of a feisty Braveheart valiantly fighting the Sassenachs (also known as Intel and Microsoft).

Table 4-2: The I²M matrix

	Asynchronous text	Synchronous text	File transfer	Telnet	Audio	Video	Newswire	Search engine	Virtual reality
Atmospherics									
Employees									
Litter									
News stories									
Signs									
Personal experiences									
Advertising									
Word of mouth									
Public relations									
Products and services									
Popular culture									

1. http://www.cba.uga.edu/~rwatson/iim/

Because we often learn by modeling the behavior of others, linking I²M cells to existing Web examples assists managers in identifying opportunities for their organization. Furthermore, by providing a variety of examples for each cell, creative behavior is aroused because each example can be a different stimulus.

News stories

Traditionally, organizations have relied on news media and advertisements to transmit their stories to the customer. Naturally, the use of intermediaries can pose problems. For example, news stories, not reported as envisaged, can result in the customer receiving a distorted, unintended message. When dealing with the Pentium hullabaloo, Intel's CEO Andy Grove used the Internet to communicate directly with customers by posting its press release to its Web page, as does Reebok.

Advertising

The hyperlink, a key feature of the Web, permits a reader to jump to another Web site by clicking on a link. An advertiser can place hyperlink signs or logos at relevant points on the Web so that interested readers may be enticed to link to the advertiser's Web site. Hyperlinks are the billboards of the information highway. They are most valuable when they appear on Web pages read by many potential consumers, such as CNN or *USA Today*. As it is very easy to record the number of links from one page to another, it is relatively simple for advertisers to place a value on a particular hyperlink and for the owners of these pages to demand an appropriate rent.

A marriage made on the Web—that's some bull!

Success in the $20 billion (€18 billion) dairy farming business is frequently determined by matching a herd of cows with the right bull. The goal is to breed cows who produce a lot of milk, and the right bull can make a lot of difference.

Consequently, a Virginia software company has developed an Internet-based service that matches a herd with a database of 1,000 bulls. The service considers factors such as parental history and milk quality. It also is programmed to avoid inbreeding, which can reduce the milk production of offspring.

Adapted from alt.cw, 1998, Web yields best of breed, *Computerworld*, Nov 23, 84.

Atmospherics

A Web site is the information age's extension of society's long history of developing attractive artificial environments. It parallels the Greek temple and Gothic cathedral of past centuries. These buildings were designed to evoke certain feelings within visitors (e.g., reverence). Similarly, a Web site should achieve a specific emotional effect on the visitor that prolongs browsing of a site.

Alberto's nightclub in Mountain View, California, stimulates interest by creating an aura of excitement and action. The visual on its home page exudes the ethos of the club. The Web provides an opportunity for customers to experience an organization's atmospherics without actually being there.

Employees

E-mail and bulletin boards have become effective methods of communicating with employees, particularly for highly dispersed international organizations. Because policy changes can be distributed inexpensively and instantly, the organization can gain a high degree of consistency in its communications with employees and other stakeholders. Instead of an in-house newsletter, an intranet can be used to keep employees informed of company developments. Previous issues of the newsletter can be made available, perhaps via a search engine, and there can be links to other related articles. For example, a story on new health benefits can have links to the firm's benefits policy manual.

Use of e-mail and the Web should lead to consistent internal communication, a necessary prerequisite of consistent external communication with customers, suppliers, shareholders, and other parties. A well-informed employee is likely to feel greater involvement with the organization and more able to perform effectively.

Litter

The discarded Big Mac wrapper blowing across the highway does little for MacDonald's corporate image. On the Internet, an advertisement arriving along with other e-mail may be perceived by some readers as highly offensive electronic pollution. Sending junk e-mail, also known as spamming, has aroused the ire of many Internet users, and America Online has taken action to block e-mail from certain firms and accounts. Just as offensive to some Web surfers are large or inappropriate graphics. These can be time polluters— wasting time and bandwidth as they load. Organizations need to ensure that their Internet communications are not offensive or time-wasting to visitors.

The Web makes it easy for unhappy consumers to create a Web site disparaging a company or product. A disgruntled Ford owner has created a Web site for the Association of Flaming Ford Owners. Consequently, firms must monitor such sites and Internet traffic about them to head off PR disasters.

Signs

Most organizations prominently display their logos and other identifying signs on their buildings, packaging, and other visual points of customer contact. There has been a clear transfer of this concept to the Web. A corporate logo frequently is visually reinforced by placing it on each Web page.

Organizations can be extremely creative in their use of signs. Reykjavik Advertising, with a collection of pages for a variety of Icelandic clients, makes clever use of the puffin, Iceland's national bird. Reykjavik Advertising's so-called traffic puffin indicates movement relative to a page hierarchy—back, up, or forward, respectively (see Figure 4-2). It is an interesting alternative to the bland arrows of a Web browser. The traffic puffin appears on each page. After viewing the pages, a clear impression of the resourceful use of the puffin remains. A new medium creates opportunities for reinventing signs.

Figure 4-2. Innovative use of a sign

Animation is another way firms can reinvent their signs. Manheim Auctions, the Atlanta-headquartered car auction firm, uses animation to reinforce recognition of its corporate logo. The inner part of its circular logo rotates. Animation catches the eye and makes the visitor more aware of the Manheim logo.

Personal experience

Customers often prefer to try products before buying, and some software providers take advantage of this preference. Qualcomm widely distributes a freeware version of Eudora Light, an e-mail package. Customers who adopt the freeware version can easily upgrade to a commercial version, which offers some appealing additional features. In Qualcomm's case, the incentive for the customer to upgrade is increased functionality.

Another approach is taken by game maker Storm Impact, which distributes TaskMaker as freeware. The full functionality of the game is available to play the first two tasks; however, the next eight tasks require payment of $25 (€23). On receipt of payment, a registration code to unlock the remaining tasks is e-mailed so that the next task can be tackled immediately. These examples support the notion of sampling—something which has previously been very difficult in the case of services and less tangible products.

Word of mouth

Gossip and idle chatter around the water fountain are now complemented by e-mail and bulletin boards. The impact of these electronic media can be quite profound as Intel discovered when the flaw in the Pentium chip was revealed in a message on the Internet. The incident was quickly conveyed to millions of Pentium customers, who bombarded Intel with e-mail. Word of mouth does not adequately describe the situation when a single electronic message can reach

> ### Carwars is now showing!
>
> Car companies and dealers and not just competing with each other for a share of the $1 trillion (€910 billion) market for new and used vehicles, financing, and insurance. With on-line car-buying services taking a piece of the pie, the companies and dealers are fighting back with on-line services of their own.
>
> Companies such as General Motors Corp., Ford Motor Co., and DaimlerChrysler are setting up their own sites and bypassing the car-buying services, which they feel are now unnecessary. The companies can provide proprietary information that is unavailable to the services. This information includes details of their incentive plans and dealer inventories including availability of requested colors and design features. Ford is using its Web site to sell used lease cars instead of putting them through auctions.
>
> The services companies are retaliating. They claim that they offer the potential buyer an overview of the entire car market. Microsoft's CarPoint provides information and product offers tailored to each vehicle so that the owner will receive e-mail reminders regarding oil changes, part replacements, and recall notices. Autoweb's site allows customers to schedule services on-line, receive advice from mechanics, and provides a service library set up by Pep Boys. Autobytel offers a Wishlist Garage so it can e-mail a customer when a car of interest becomes available.
>
> Adapted from Warner, F. 1999. Online battle starts to heat up over sales of cars to U.S. drivers. *The Wall Street Journal Interactive Edition*, Feb. 18.

hundreds of thousands of people in a matter of minutes. It's more like a tsunami gathering momentum and crashing on the corporate doorstep before managers realize even a ripple of discontent. Bad news travels extremely fast on the Internet. News is not always bad; Land's End publishes customers' testimonials about its products.

Corporations need to monitor bulletin boards that discuss their products and those of their competitors. As a result, they can quickly detect emerging problems and respond to assertions that may be incorrect. Eavesdropping on customers' conversations is an important source of market intelligence, and it is becoming an important element of public relations.

Public relations

When IBM announced its takeover bid for Lotus, it used the Internet to reach its stakeholders, media, and Lotus employees. Once the financial markets had been notified, IBM's Web page featured the letter from IBM CEO Louis Gerstner to Jim Manzi, Lotus CEO. Also included were the internal memo to IBM employees, press release, audio clip of Gerstner explaining the offer, and a transcript of Gerstner's 45-minute news conference. By the end of the day, 23,000 people had accessed the Web page—about double the normal traffic. In contrast, Lotus's page had a four-paragraph statement from Manzi, and a company spokesperson said Lotus would respond when it had more to say about the offer.

As IBM demonstrated, the Web can be an effective public relations tool. The advantage is that a company can immediately transmit its message to stakeholders without relying on intermediaries, such as newspapers and TV, to redistribute messages. Of course, mass mailing is also a method for directly reaching stakeholders, but a letter lacks the recency and multimedia features of the Web.

Products and services

There are now thousands of firms using the Internet to deliver products and services. Software companies are selling software directly from Web sites (e.g., Adobe sells fonts) and many companies deliver services via their Web site (e.g., UPS permits customers to track parcels).

Computer firms struggle to solve hardware and software problems for a multitude of customers. This is a problem that can easily spiral out of control. One approach is to let customers solve each other's problems. As sure as there is one customer with a problem, there is another who has solved it or who would love the opportunity to tackle a puzzler. If customers can be convinced to solve each other's problems, then this creates the possibility of lowering the cost of customer service and raising customer satisfaction levels.

Thus, the real task is to ensure that the customer with the problem finds the customer with the solution. Apple, like many hardware and software firms, has a simple system for improving customer service. It uses a listserv to network customers using similar products. As a result, the customers support each other, reducing the number of people that Apple has to support.

Popular culture

Firms have discovered that popular culture (including movies, songs, and live performances) can be used to publicize their goods. As the Internet develops, clearly labeled products and ads are appearing in virtual network games. A popular MUD, Genocide, already features well-known fast-food stores. Goalkeeper, an Internet soccer simulator, lets visitors kick a soccer ball to try to beat the goalkeeper. The background of the game, a soccer stadium, includes typical sports arena advertising, including a banner for ABN AMRO, one of the world's top 20 banks.

> ### Benetton: a case study of I²M
>
> Some organizations have intuitively grasped the central theme of the I²M model. Benetton, for instance, uses several Internet technologies and, with a different twist on integrated communication, uses its Web site to communicate with a variety of stakeholders (customers, investors, journalists, and store owners). The most obvious characteristic of the Benetton Web site is its reinforcement of the Benetton image. The United Colors of Benetton logo on every page is echoed in the images and fonts used for signage. Benetton goes a step further in reinventing signs; its distinctive ads are used to convey the purpose of a page. For example, the feedback page, where visitors provide comments to Benetton about the site, has a Benetton ad—a nun kissing a priest—at the top of the page.
>
> In a variation on word of mouth, Benetton publishes e-mail that is critical of the company's ads. As well as listing customers' complaints about displeasing ads, Benetton has a hypertext link to the offending ad so that the Web visitor can make a personal judgment. Again, this fits with Benetton's somewhat confrontational, in-your-face advertising.
>
> The Benetton site is a source of considerable information. The advertising index lists Benetton ads, providing both low and high resolution images. All press releases since 1993 are available, and journalists can sign up to receive electronic copies of future releases. Investors can download a copy of the financial report. A search engine provides rapid access to available information.
>
> Perhaps the ultimate weapon for establishing atmospherics is virtual reality. Visitors can stand in the middle of a Benetton store and look around and vicariously experience the look and feel of a typical Benetton retail outlet. Visitors are also invited on a virtual excursion to a Benetton factory and the corporate headquarters. Atmospherics dominate the design of the Benetton Web site. For the clothing industry, where brand image can be so valuable, this emphasis is imperative. The Web site is a carefully crafted integration of Internet tools to promote the Benetton image.

Conclusion

As transactions are increasingly conducted electronically, a firm's Web site will be its defining image and the main point of interaction with many stakeholders. Consequently, firms must ensure that they take full advantage of the technology available to maximize their impact. A systematic approach, using the I²M matrix and modeling the behavior of others, provides a framework for designing and implementing an effective Web site that takes full advantage of the Internet tools. Integrated use of this technology, however, is not enough. An enterprise, with a jumble of different page layouts and icons, communicates disorganization. The collective image of the Web site must communicate the overall integration and message of the organization. Not only must use of Internet tools be integrated, but also a corporation's entire Web presence must be cohesive in order to communicate a consistent message to stakeholders.

Cases

Subirana, B., and S. Palavecino. 1998. *Amadeus: starting on the Internet and electronic commerce*. Barcelona, Spain: IESE. ECCH 198-024-1.

References

Schultz, D. E., S. I. Tannenbaum, and R. F. Lauterborn. 1994. *The new marketing paradigm: integrated marketing communications*. Lincolnwood, IL: NTC Business Books.

Zinkhan, G. M., and R. T. Watson. 1996. Advertising trends: innovation and the process of creative destruction. *Journal of Business Research* 37 (3):163-171.

5

Promotion & purchase: Measuring effectiveness

Introduction

The Web has attracted a great deal of attention in recent years—perhaps significantly, in the influential business press and popular culture. Uniform Resource Locators (URLs) appear in many advertisements, and *Business Week* devotes a page to listing the URLs of its advertisers.[1]

Reporting on the Web is currently fascinating to general readers and listing URLs is helpful to consumers. However, systematic research is required to reveal the true nature of commerce on the Web. This is true particularly from the perspective of the Web in marketing communication, and especially so for the Web as an advertising medium or tool. In this chapter, we provide a brief overview of the Web as a phenomenon of the late 20th century; then we explore the Web as an advertising medium, using established theoretical models of consumer and industrial buying behavior; finally, we develop a model of Web conversion efficiency—its power to move the customer from being a passive Internet surfer to an interactive user of the medium.

The Internet and the World Wide Web

Cyberspace, or to give it its less clichéd name, the Internet (the *net*), is a new medium based on broadcasting and publishing. However, unlike traditional broadcast media, it facilitates two-way communication between actors; unlike most personal selling (telemarketing being the obvious exception), it is not physically face to face, but neither is it time-bound. The medium possesses interactivity—it has the facility for individuals and organizations to communicate directly with one another regardless of distance or time. The Web has introduced a much broader audience to the net. Furthermore, it allows anyone (organization or individual) to have a 24-hour-a-day presence on the Internet.

---

1. This chapter is based on Berthon, P. R., L. F. Pitt, and R. T. Watson. 1996. The World Wide Web as an advertising medium: towards an understanding of conversion efficiency. *Journal of Advertising Research* 36 (1):43-54.

The Web is not a transient phenomenon. It warrants serious attention by business practitioners. Statistics support this, although one astute observer recommends strongly that all estimates be made in pencil only, as the growth is so rapid. No communication medium or electronic technology, not even fax or personal computers, has ever grown as quickly.

An electronic trade show and a virtual flea market

While most academics and practitioners might be starting to think about, and even acknowledge, the importance of a Web site as a marketing communication tool, to date little systematic research has been conducted into the nature and effectiveness of this medium. Most of the work done so far has been of a descriptive nature—"what the medium is," using such surrogate measures as the size of the Web audience to indicate its potential. While these endeavors might add to our general understanding, they do not address more specific issues of concern, such as the communication objectives that advertisers might have, and how they expect Web sites to achieve these objectives. Neither do these studies assess the effectiveness of this new medium from the perspective of the recipient of the message (the *buyer*, to use the broadest marketing term).

The Web is rather like a cross between an electronic trade show and a community flea market. As an **electronic trade show**, it can be thought of as a giant international exhibition hall where potential buyers can enter at will and visit prospective sellers. Like a trade show, they may do this passively, by simply wandering around, enjoying the sights and sounds, pausing to pick up a pamphlet or brochure here, and a sticker, key ring, or sample there. Alternatively, they may become vigorously interactive in their search for information and want-satisfaction, by talking to fellow attendees, actively seeking the booths of particular exhibitors, carefully examining products, soliciting richer information, and even engaging in sales transactions with the exhibitor. The basic ingredients are still the same. As a **flea market**, it possesses the fundamental characteristics of openness, informality, and interactivity, a combination of a community and a marketplace or marketspace. A flea market is an alternative forum that offers the consumer an additional search option, which may provide society with a model for constructing more satisfying and adaptive marketplace options. The Web has much in common with a flea market.

The central and fundamental problem facing conventional trade show and flea marketers is how to convert visitors, casually strolling around the exhibition center or market, into customers at best, or leads at least. Similarly, a central dilemma confronting the Web advertiser is how to turn surfers (those who browse the Web) into interactors (attracting the surfers to the extent that they become interested; ultimately purchasers; and, staying interactive, repeat purchasers). An excellent illustration of a Web site as electronic trade show or flea market is to be found at the site established by Security First Network

Bank, which was one of the first financial services institutions to offer full-service banking on the Internet. The company uses the graphic metaphor of a conventional bank to communicate and interact with potential and existing customers, including an electronic inquiries desk, electronic brochures for general information, and electronic tellers to deal with routine transactions. Thus, the degree of interaction is dependent on the individual surfer—those merely interested can take an electronic stroll through the bank, while those desiring more information can find it. Customers can interact to whatever degree they wish—transfer funds, make payments, write electronic checks, talk with electronic tellers (where they are always first in line), and see the electronic bank manager for additional requests, complaints, and general feedback.

We have taken the notion of trade shows as a marketing communication tool and extended it to the possible role of the Web site as an advertising medium. This is speculated upon, in the context of both the buying and selling process stages, and in both industrial and consumer contexts, in Figure 5-1. The relative (to mass advertising and personal selling) communication effectiveness of a Web site is questioned graphically in Figure 5-1, although without prior quantitative data, it is mere conjecture at this stage to posit a profile. By simply placing a question mark between mass advertising and personal selling in the figure, we tempt the reader to contemplate the communication profile of the Web. Industrial buying can be thought of as the series of stages in the first column in Figure 5-1. The buyer's information needs differ at each stage, as do the tasks of the marketing communicator. In column 2, a model of the steps in the consumer decision making process for complex purchases is shown, and it will be seen that these overlap the steps in the buying phases model to a considerable extent. The tasks that confront the advertiser and the seller in both industrial and consumer markets can similarly be mapped against these stages, through a series of communication objectives. This is shown in column 3. Each of these objectives requires different communication tasks of the seller, and these are similarly outlined in column 4. So, for example, generating awareness of a new product might be most effectively achieved through broadcast advertising, while closing a sale would best be achieved face to face, in a selling transaction. Most marketers, in both consumer and business-to-business markets, employ a mix of communication tools to achieve various objectives in the marketing communication process, judiciously combining advertising and personal selling.

The relative cost-effectiveness of advertising and personal selling in performing marketing communication tasks depends on the stage of the buying process, with personal selling becoming more cost effective the closer the buyer gets to the latter phases in the purchasing sequence—this is shown in column 5. A central question then is where does a Web site fit in terms of communication effectiveness? Again, rather than profile this, we leave it to the reader.

New customer/ prospect buying phase	Complex consumer buying process	Key seller communication objectives and tasks		Relative communication effectiveness
		Communication objectives	Task	
1. Need recognition	1. Awareness of needs	Generate awareness	Prospecting	
2. Developing product specifications	2. Information processing	Feature comprehension	Opening relationship, qualifying prospect	
3. Search and evaluation of suppliers	3. Evaluation processing	Lead generation	Qualifying prospect	
4. Evaluation	4. Purchase decision	Performance comprehension	Presenting sales message	
5. Supplier selection	5. Purchase	Negotiation of terms/Offer customization	Closing sale	
6. Purchase feedback	6. Post-purchase evaluation	Reassurance	Account service	

Figure 5-1. Buying and selling and Web marketing communication

At this point, we re-emphasize the fact that the Web is still in its infancy, which means that no identifiable attempts have so far appeared in scholarly journals that methodically clarify its anticipated role and performance. This deficiency probably stems from the fact that few organizations or individuals have even begun to spell out their objectives in operating a Web site, let alone quantified them. This is not entirely unexpected—unlike expenditure on broadcast advertising, or the long-term financial commitment to a sales force, the establishment of a Web site is a relatively inexpensive venture, from which retraction is easy and rapid. It is not unlikely that many advertisers are on the Web simply because it is relatively quick and easy, and because they fear that the consequences of not having a presence will outweigh whatever might be the outcomes of a hastily ill-conceived presence. This lack of clear and quantified objectives, understanding, and the absence of a unified framework for evaluating performance, have compelled decision makers to rely on intuition, imitation, and advertising experience when conceptualizing, developing, designing, and implementing Web sites.

These two concerns—the lack of clear or consistent objectives and the relationship of those objectives to the variables under the control of the firm—are the issues that engage us here. We propose a more direct assessment of Web site performance using multiple indices such that differing Web site objectives can be directly translated into appropriate performance measures. We then explicitly link these performance measures to tactical variables under the control of the firm and present a conceptual framework to relate several of the most frequently mentioned objectives of Web site participation to measures of performance associated with Web site traffic flow. Finally, we develop a set of models linking the tactical variables to six performance measures that Web advertisers and marketers can use to measure the effectiveness and performance against objectives of a Web site. Finally, we discuss normative implications and suggest areas for further development.

The role of the Web in the marketing communication mix

Personal selling is usually the largest single item in the industrial marketing communications mix. On the other hand, broadcast advertising is typically the dominant way used to reach consumers by marketers. Where do Web sites fit? The Web site is something of a mix between direct selling (it can engage the visitor in a dialogue) and advertising (it can be designed to generate awareness, explain/demonstrate the product, and provide information—without interactive involvement). It can play a cost-effective role in the communication mix, in the early stages of the process-need recognition, development of product specifications, and supplier search, but can also be useful as the buying process progresses toward evaluation and selection. Finally, the site is also cost-effective in providing feedback on product/service performance. Web sites might typically be viewed as complementary to the direct selling activity by industrial marketers, and as supplementary to advertising by consumer marketers. For example, Web sites can be used to:

- gain access to previously unknown or inaccessible buying influences. Cathay Pacific Airlines uses a Web site to interview frequent international airline flyers, and determine their preferences with regard to airline, destination, airport, and even aircraft. Much of the active ticket purchasing is not normally done by these individuals, but by a secretary or personal assistant acting on their behalf.

- project a favorable corporate image. Guinness allows surfers to download from its Web site its latest television commercial, which can then be used as a screen saver. While the advertiser has not made the objectives of this strategy public, conceivably the approach builds affinity with the corporate brand as fun involvement, while the screen saver provides a constant reminder of the advertising message.

- provide product information. Many business schools are now using their Web sites to provide information on MBA and executive programs—indeed, there is now even an award to the business school judged to have the most effective Web site in North America. Similarly, Honda uses its Web site to give very detailed information about its latest models. Not only can the surfer download video footage and sound about the latest Honda cars, but by clicking the mouse on directional arrows, can get different visual perspectives of the vehicles, both from outside and inside the car.

- generate qualified leads for salespeople. The South African life assurance company SANLAM uses its Web site to identify customer queries, and if needed, can direct sales advisers to these.

- handle customer complaints, queries, and suggestions. Software developers such as Silverplatter are using their Web sites as a venue for customers to voice complaints and offer suggestions about the product. While this allows customers a facility to let off steam, it also allows the marketer to appear open to communication, and perhaps more importantly, to identify and rectify commonly occurring problems speedily.

- allows customers access to its system through its Web site. FedEx's surprisingly popular site allows customers to track their shipments traveling through the system by typing in the package receipt number. "The Web is one of the best customer relationship tools ever," according to a FedEx manager.

- serve as an electronic couponing device. A company called E-Coupon.com targets college students, because they possess two important characteristics—they are generally very computer literate and also need to save money. The site features lists of participating campus merchants, including music stores, coffee houses, and pharmacies. Students click on shop names to get a printable picture of a coupon on their computer screen, which they can take to shops for discounts or free samples; in return, they fill out a demographic profile and answer questions about product use.

In summary, different organizations may have different advertising and marketing objectives for establishing and maintaining a Web presence. One organization might wish to use the Web as a means of introducing itself and its new products to a potentially wide, international audience. Its objectives could be to create corporate and product awareness and inform the market. In this instance, the Web site can be used to expedite the buyer's progress down phases 1 and 2 in Figure 5-1. On the other hand, if the surfer knows the firm and its products, then the net dialogue can be used to propel this customer down to the lower phases in the buying progression. Another firm may be advertising and marketing well-known existing products, and its Web site objectives could be to solicit feedback from current customers as well as inform new customers.

Thus, Web sites can be used to move customers and prospects through successive phases of the buying process. They do this by first attracting surfers, making contact with interested surfers (among those attracted), qualifying/converting a portion of the interested contacts into interactive customers, and keeping these interactive customers interactive. Different tactical variables, both directly related to the Web site as well as to other elements of the marketing communication mix, will have a particular impact at different phases of this conversion process: For example, hot links (electronic links which connect a particular site to other relevant and related sites) may be critical in attracting surfers. However, once attracted, it may be the level of interactivity on the site that will be critical to making these surfers interactive. This kind of flow process is analogous to that for the adoption of new packaged goods (market share of a brand = proportion aware x proportion of new buyers given awareness x repeat purchasing rate given awareness and trial) and in organizational buying (the probability of choice is conditional on variables such as awareness, meeting specifications, and preference).

Web marketing communication: a conceptual framework

Based on the above, we model the flow of surfer activity on a Web site as a six-stage process, which is shown in Figure 5-2. The variables and measures shown in Figure 5-2 are defined in Table 5-1.

All surfers on the Web may not be the relevant target audience for a given firm. Surfers can be in one of two groups:

- those potentially interested in the organization (η_0),
- those not interested ($1-\eta_0$).

The attractiveness of having a Web site for the organization depends on $Q_0\eta_0$, the number of potentially interested surfers on the Web (where Q_0 is the net size measured in terms of surfers). The first stage of the model represents the flow of surfers on the net to land on the firm's Web site, and it is acknowledged that only a fraction of the aware surfers ($Q_0\eta_0$) visits a firm's Web site. This describes the awareness efficiency (η_0) of the Web site. The awareness efficiency measures how effectively the organization is able to make surfers aware of its Web site. Advertisers and marketers can employ reasonably common and well-known awareness-generating techniques to affect this, such as including the Web site address in all advertising and publicity, on product packaging and other corporate communication materials, such as letterheads, business cards, and brochures.

The awareness efficiency index is:

$$\text{awareness efficiency} = \eta_0 = \frac{\text{people aware of the site}}{\text{people with Web access}} = \frac{Q_1}{Q_0}$$

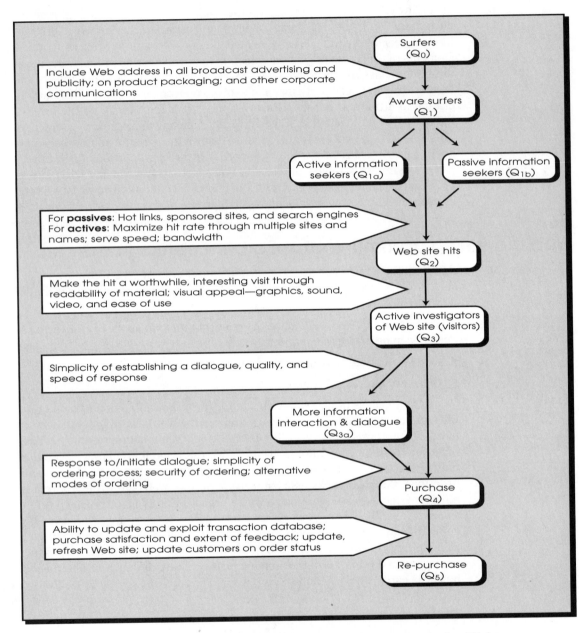

Figure 5-2. A model of the conversion process on the Web

The second stage of the model concerns attempts to get aware surfers to find the Web site. We distinguish between **active** and **passive** information seekers. Active seekers (Q_{1a}) are those who intentionally seek to hit the Web site, whereas passive seekers (Q_{1b}) are those aware surfers whose primary purpose

Table 5-1: Web efficiency variables

Variable	Meaning
Q_0	Number of people with Web access
Q_1	Number of people aware of the site
Q_2	Number of hits on the site
Q_3	Number of active visitors to the site
Q_4	Number of purchases
Q_5	Number of repurchases

in surfing was not necessarily to hit the Web site. Only a fraction of the aware surfers visit the firm's Web site. The second stage of the model thus represents the *locatability/attractability efficiency* (η_1) of the Web site. This measures how effectively the organization is able to convert aware surfers into Web site hits, either by facilitating active seeking behavior (surfers who actively look for the Web site), or by attracting passive seekers (not actively looking for the Web site, but not against finding it).

What's in a URL?

Having the right name can make all the difference to the number of visitors a Web site attracts. By purchasing the name art.com, a poster and framing store (formerly www.artuframe.com) realized a 30 percent increase in site traffic, 400,000 unique visitors per month, and has become the largest store of its type on the Web. With a merchant agreement with Yahoo!, where art.com's button appears whenever anything art related is requested, the number of hits will be sure to increase.

In addition, there are 2,800 affiliates (increasing by 350-400 per week) responsible for 20 percent of the company's revenue. This affiliate program allows art.com to get new customers at half the cost of banner advertising.

Gardner, E. 1999. Art.com. *Internet World*, Feb. 15, 13-14.

Enabling active seekers to hit the Web site easily can be achieved by maximizing the locatability of the site—such as using multiple sites (e.g., Web servers in the U.S., Europe, and Asia), names for the site that can be easily guessed (e.g., www.apple.com), and enhancing server speed and bandwidth (the number of visits which can be handled concurrently). Tools to attract passive seekers include using a large number of relevant hot links (e.g., EDS has a link from ISWorld, the Web site for information systems academics, to its Web site), embedding hot links in sponsored Web sites (e.g., IBM sponsors the Wimbledon Tennis Tournament Web site), and banner ads on search engines. We summarize the locatability/attractability index as:

$$\text{attractability efficiency} = \eta_1 = \frac{\text{hits on the site}}{\text{people aware of the site}} = \frac{Q_2}{Q_1}$$

where hits refers to the number of surfers who alight on the Web site.

At this stage, it should be apparent that there is a difference between a *hit* and a *visit*. Merely hitting or landing on a site does not mean that the surfer did anything with the information to be found there—the surfer might simply hit and move on. A visit, as compared to a hit, implies greater interaction between the surfer and the Web page. It may mean spending appreciable time (i.e., $> x$ minutes) reading the page. Alternatively, it could be completing a form or querying a database. Although the operational definition of a visit is to some extent dependent on the content and detail on the page, the overriding distinctive feature of a visit is some interaction between the surfer and the Web page.

The next phase of the model concerns the efficiency and ability of the Web site in converting the hit to a visit. The third stage of our model represents the *contact efficiency* (η_2) of the Web site. This measures how effectively the organization transforms Web site hits into visits. The efforts of the advertiser at this stage should be focused on turning a hit into a worthwhile visit. Thus, the hit should be interesting, hold the visitor's attention, and persuade them to stay awhile to browse. The material should be readable—the concept of readability is a well-established principle in advertising communication. Visual effects should be appealing—sound and video can hold interest as well as inform. The possibility of gaining something, such as winning a prize in a competition, may be effective. The interface should be easy and intuitive. We summarize the contact efficiency index as:

$$\text{contact efficiency} = \eta_2 = \frac{\text{active visitors to the site}}{\text{hits on the site}} = \frac{Q_3}{Q_2}$$

Once the visitor is engaged—in real time—in a visit at the Web site, he or she should be able to do one or both of the following:

- establish a dialogue (at the simplest level, this may be signing an electronic visitors' book; at higher levels, this may entail e-mail requests for information). The visitors' book at the Robert Mondavi Wineries' Web site not only allows visitors to complete a questionnaire and thus receive very attractive promotional material, including a recipe brochure, it also allows the more inquisitive visitor to ask specific questions by e-mail. It is important to note that it is feasible to establish the dialogue in a way that elicits quite detailed information from the visitor—for example, by offering the visitor the opportunity to participate in a competition in exchange for information in the form of an electronic survey, or by promising a reward for interaction (the recipe booklet in the preceding example).

- place an order. This may be facilitated by ensuring simplicity of the ordering process, providing a secure means of payment, as well as options on mode of payment (e.g., credit card, check, electronic transfer of funds). Alternative ordering methods might also be provided (e.g., telephone, e-mail, or a postal order form that can be downloaded and printed). For example, the electronic music store CDnow offers a huge variety of CDs and other items such as tapes and video cassettes. It provides visitors with thousands of reviews from the well-respected *All-Music Guide* as well as thousands of artists' biographies. A powerful program built into the site allows a search for recordings by artist, title, and key words. It also tells about an artist's musical influences and lists other performers in the same genre. Each name is hotlinked so that a mouse click connects the visitor to even more information. CDnow's seemingly endless layers of sub-directories makes it easy and fun to get lost in a world of information, education, and entertainment—precisely the ingredients for inducing flow through the model. More importantly, from a measurability perspective, the site converts some of its many visitors to buyers.

This capability to turn visitors into purchasers, we term conversion efficiency, and summarize it in the form of an index as follows:

$$\text{conversion efficiency} = \eta_3 = \frac{\text{purchases}}{\text{active visitors}} = \frac{Q_4}{Q_3}$$

The final stage in the process entails converting purchases into re-purchases. The firm should consider the proficiency of the Web site not only to create purchases, but to turn these buyers into loyal customers who revisit the site and purchase on an ongoing basis. Variables which the marketer can influence include:

- regular updating and refreshing of the Web site. It is more likely that customers will revisit a Web site that is regularly revised and kept current;

- soliciting purchase satisfaction and feedback to improve the product specifically, and interaction generally;

- regular updating and exploiting of the transaction database. Once captured, customer data becomes a strategic asset, which can be used to further refine and retarget electronic marketing efforts. This can take a number of forms: customers can be reminded electronically to repurchase (e.g., an e-mail to a customer to have a car serviced); customers can be invited to collaborate with the marketer (e.g., loyal customers can be rewarded for referrals by supplying the e-mail addresses of friends or colleagues who may be leads).

This capability to turn purchasers into repurchasers, we term retention efficiency, and summarize as follows:

$$\text{retention efficiency} = \eta_4 = \frac{\text{repurchases}}{\text{purchases}} = \frac{Q_5}{Q_4}$$

Customer retention

On-line retailers are trying different methods of encouraging customers to come back and buy again. With an average cost of \$34 (€31) to get a new customer, retention has become an important focus.

Cyberian Outpost Inc., an on-line computer retailer, is improving customer retention by tracking user behavior and analyzing patterns of activity to target customers by geography, demographics, and past purchases. This led to two successful direct e-mail promotion offers.

CDnow Inc. launched a frequent-buyer program in October 1998. Under the scheme, points are awarded for purchases and can then be later redeemed for purchases. The company also used Net Perceptions Inc.'s GroupLens *recommendation engine*, which matches the customer's tastes with those of other customers, to offer suggestions for other purchases.

Barnesandnoble.com is using Net Perceptions to personalize its service. It has also expanded its optional e-mail announcement program, where customers can request mailings about new titles by category or author.

Adapted from Machlis, S. 1999. Web retailers try their hits up. *Computerworld*, Feb. 8, 48.

Finally, we define a sixth, or overall average Web site efficiency index (η_{Av}), which can be thought of as a summary of the process outlined in Figure 5-1.

$$\text{Web site efficiency} = \eta_{Av} = \frac{1}{5}\sum_{1}^{5}\frac{Q_n}{Q_{n-1}}$$

This index can be an effective way to establish the extent to which Web site advertising and marketing objectives have been met. The measure is particularly relevant for a Web direct mail order operation where the main objective is to generate purchases and repeat purchases. However, a simple average may in other cases be misleading, and a more refined and appropriate measure might be a weighted average. A weighted average index is defined below:

$$\eta_{WAv} = \frac{1}{5}\sum_{1}^{5}\frac{Q_n}{Q_{n-1}} \cdot \mu_i$$

where μ_i is the weighting accorded to each of the five efficiency indices in the model. So, for example, some advertisers might regard visits to the Web site as a very important criterion of its success (objective), without wishing or expecting these visits to necessarily result directly in sales. Other advertisers and marketers might want the visit to result in dialogue, which could result in sales, but only indirectly—mailing or faxing further information, accepting a free product sample, or requesting a sales call. Another group of Web advertisers might wish to emphasize retention efficiency. They would want to use the Web as a medium for establishing dialogue with existing customers and facilitating routine reordering. It would therefore be useful for advertisers and marketers wishing to establish overall Web efficiency to be able to weight Web objectives in terms of their relative importance.

Caching and undercounting

The previously developed model assumes that all hits are counted. However, there are hits that are never detected by a Web server because pages can be read from a cache memory rather than the server. A cache is temporary memory designed to speed up access to a data source. In the case of the Web, pages previously retrieved may be stored on the disk (the cache in this case) of the personal computer running the browser. Thus, when a person is flipping back and forth between previously retrieved pages, the browser retrieves the required pages from the local disk rather than the remote server. The use of a cache speeds up retrieval, reduces network traffic, and decreases the load on the server. As a consequence, however, data collected by a Web server undercount hits. The extent of undercounting depends on the form of caching.

Netscape, one of the most popular browsers, offers three levels of caching: *once per session*, *always*, and *never*. In terms of undercounting, the worst situation is *never*, which implies that if the page is in cache, the browser will not retrieve a new version from the server. This also means the customer could be viewing a page that could be months out of date. *Always* means the browser always checks to ensure that the latest version is about to be displayed. A hit will not be recorded if the page in the cache is the current version. The default for Netscape, *once per session*, results in undercounting but does mean the customer is reading current information, unless that page changes during the session.

The existence of a *proxy server* can further exacerbate undercounting. A proxy server is essentially a cache memory for a group of users (e.g., department, organization, or even country). Requests from a browser to a Web server are first routed to a proxy server, which keeps a copy of pages it has retrieved and distributed to the browsers attached to it. When any browser served by the proxy issues a request for a page, the proxy server will return the page if it is already in its memory rather than retrieve the page from the original server. For instance, a company could operate a proxy server to improve response time for company personnel. Although dozens of people within the organization may reference a particular Web page, the originating server may score one hit per day for the company because of the intervening proxy server. To further complicate matters, there can be layers of proxy servers, and one page retrieved from the original Web server may end up being seen by thousands of people within a nation. Clearly, the proliferation of proxy servers, which is likely to happen as the Web extends, will result in severe undercounting.

The use of cache memory or proxy servers will result in undercounting of hits (Q_2) and active visitors (Q_3). Consequently, the locatability/attractability index (η_1) will be underestimated since Q_2 is the numerator in the index's equation, and the conversion efficiency index (η_3) will be overestimated as Q_3 is in the denominator. It is more difficult to conjecture the effect on the contact efficiency index (η_2). One possibility is that the index is underestimated because active visitors browse the site more frequently than those who just hit, and as a result are more likely to read the page from cache memory.

Clearly, empirical research is required to estimate correction factors for η_1, η_2, and η_3. Unfortunately, these correction factors are likely to differ by page and change over time as the distribution of proxy servers changes. Therefore, the initial perception that the Web enables the ready calculation of efficiency measures needs to be tempered by the recognition that cache memory can distort the situation.

The counting problem caused by caching is not unlike other counting problems encountered by advertisers. Viewership, listenership, and readership of conventional media are cases in point. The issue of readership, for example, has perplexed advertisers, researchers, and publishers for many years: How does one measure readership? Is it merely circulation? Circulation probably undercounts in one way, because there may be more than one reader (e.g., two people read the subscription to *Wired*), or overcounts in another (e.g., no one reads the subscription). We thus believe that caching is a new variation of the same old counting problem, and creative managers will need to discover innovative ways to solve it.

Conclusion

A fundamental problem in researching the effectiveness of marketing mix variables, such as pricing strategy or advertising, is that of isolating them from others. This is compounded further when the effects of a variable can be indirect, or have a prolonged lag effect. Cases in point are advertising's ability to create awareness, which might or might not lead to an immediate sale, and its lag effects—consumers remember slogans long after campaigns have ended, and the effects of this on sales continue to intrigue researchers. Thus, advertisers and marketers sustain their efforts in searching for ways in which returns to marketing investments generally, and communication capital in particular, can be enhanced. This highlights the importance of establishing specific communication objectives for Web sites, and for identifying measurable means of determining the success of Web ventures. There is perhaps some solace to be gained from realizing that the Web is a lot more *measurable* than many other marketing communication efforts, with feedback being relatively quick, if not immediate.

The Web is a new medium which is characterized by ease of entry, relatively low set-up costs, globalness, time independence, and interactivity. As such, it represents a remarkable new opportunity for advertisers and marketers to communicate with new and existing markets in a very integrated way. Many advertisers will use it to achieve hitherto undreamed-of success; for others, it will be an opportunity lost and a damp squib. We hope that the process model for assessing Web site efficiency will achieve more of the former condition. From an academic perspective, the model can be used to develop research propositions concerning the maximization of Web site efficiency, and using data from real Web sites, to test these propositions. For the practitioner, the model provides a sequence of productivity measures which can be calibrated with relative ease. The challenges facing both parties, however, is to maximize the creativity that will justify advertising and marketing investments in a Web presence.

Cases

Roos, J., M. Lissack, and D. Oliver. 1998. *Bringing the Internet to the masses: America Online Inc. (AOL)*. Lausanne, Switzerland: IMD. ECCH 398-184-1.

Christiaanse, E., J. Been, and T. van Diepen. 1997. *KLM Cargo "bringing worlds together"* Breukelen, Netherlands: Nijenrode University. ECCH 397-067-1.

References

Blattberg, R. C., and J. Deighton. 1991. Interactive marketing: exploiting the age of addressability. *Sloan Management Review* 33 (1):5-14.

Gopalakrishna, S., and G. L. Lilien. 1995. A three-stage model of industrial trade show performance. *Marketing Science* 14 (1):22-42.

Rayport, Jeffrey F., and John J. Sviokla. 1994. Managing in marketspace. *Harvard Business Review* 72 (6):141-150.

Sherry, J. F. 1990. A sociocultural analysis of a midwestern American flea market. *Journal of Consumer Research* 17 (1):13-30.

6
Distribution
• • • • • •

Introduction

The Internet and the Web will radically change distribution. The new medium undermines key assumptions upon which traditional distribution philosophy is based, and in practice renders many conventional channels and intermediaries obsolete.

In simple markets of old, producers of goods or services dealt directly with the consumers of those offerings. In some modern business-to-business markets, suppliers also interact on a face-to-face basis with their customers. However, in most contemporary markets, mass production and mass consumption have caused intermediaries to enter the junction between buyer and seller. These intermediaries have either taken title to the goods or services in their flow from producer to customer, or have, in some way, facilitated this by their specialization in one or more of the functions that have to occur for such movement to occur. These flows of title and functions and the intermediaries who have facilitated them have generally come to be known as distribution channels. For a majority of marketing decision makers, dealing with the channel for their product or service ranks as one of the key marketing quandaries faced. In many cases, despite what the textbooks have suggested, there is frequently no real decision as to *who* should constitute the channel—rather, it is a question of how best to deal with the incumbent channel. Marketing channel decisions are also critical because they intimately affect all other marketing and overall strategic decisions. Distribution channels generally involve relatively long-term commitments, but if managed effectively over time, they create a key external resource. Small wonder then that they exhibit powerful inertial tendencies, for once they are in place and working well, managers are reluctant to fix what is not broken. We contend that the Web will change distribution like no other environmental force since the industrial revolution. Not only will it modify many of the assumptions on which distribution channel structure is based, in many cases, it will transform and even obliterate channels themselves. In doing so, it will render many intermediaries obsolete, while simultaneously creating new channels and, indeed, new intermediaries.

First, we review some of the rationale for distribution channel structure and identify the key tasks of a distribution channel. Second, we consider the Internet and the Web, and describe three forces that will affect the fundamental functions of distribution channels. This then enables the construction of a technology-distribution function matrix, which we suggest is a powerful tool for managers to use to assess the impact that electronic commerce will have on their channels of distribution. Next, we visit each of the cells in this matrix and present a very brief case of a channel in which the medium is currently affecting distribution directly. Finally, we conclude by identifying some of the long-term effects of technology on distribution channels, and possible avenues for management to explore to minimize the detrimental consequences for their distribution strategies specifically, and for overall corporate strategy in general.

What is the purpose of a distribution strategy?

The purpose of a distribution channel is to make the *right* quantities of the right product/service available at the *right* place, at the *right* time. What has made distribution strategy unique relative to the other marketing mix decisions is that it has been almost entirely dependent on physical location. The old saying among retailers is that the three keys to success are the 3 Ls— *Location, Location, Location!*

Intermediaries provide economies of distribution by increasing the efficiency of the process. They do this by creating time, place, and possession utility, or what we have referred to simply as right product, right place, right time. Intermediaries in the distribution channel fulfill three basic functions.

1. Intermediaries support economies of scope by **adjusting the discrepancy of assortments**. Producers supply large quantities of a relatively small assortment of products or services, while customers require relatively small quantities of a large assortment of products and services. By performing the functions of sorting and assorting, intermediaries create possession utility through the process of exchange and also create time and place utilities. We refer to these activities as *reassortment/sorting*, which comprise:

    *   **Sorting** which consists of arranging products or services according to class, kind, or size.

    *   **Sorting out** which would refine sorting by, for example, grading products or output.

    *   **Accumulation** which involves the aggregation of stocks from different suppliers, such as all (or the major) producers of household equipment or book publishers.

- **Allocation** which is really distribution according to a plan—who will get what the producer(s) produced. This might typically involve an activity such as *breaking bulk*.

- **Assorting** which has to do with putting an appropriate *package* together. Thus, a men's outfitter might provide an assortment of suitable clothing: shirts, ties, trousers, socks, shoes, and underclothes.

2. Intermediaries **routinize** transactions so that the cost of distribution can be minimized. Because of this *routinization*, transactions do not need to be bargained on an individual basis, which would tend to be inefficient in most markets. Routinization facilitates exchange by leading to standardization and automation. Standardization of products and services enables comparison and assessment, which in turn abets the production of the most highly valued items. By the standardization of issues, such as lot size, delivery frequency, payment, and communication, a routine is created to make the exchange relationship between buyers and sellers both effective and efficient. In channels where it has been possible to automate activities, the costs of activities such as reordering can be minimized—for example, the automatic placing of an order when inventories reach a certain minimum level. In essence, automation involves machines or systems performing tasks previously performed by humans—thereby eliminating errors and reducing labor costs.

3. Intermediaries facilitate the **searching** processes of both producers and customers by structuring the information essential to both parties. Sellers are searching for buyers and buyers are searching for sellers, and at the simplest level, intermediaries provide a place for these parties to find each other. *Searching* occurs because of uncertainty. Producers are not positive about customers' needs and customers cannot be sure that they will be able to satisfy their consumption needs. Intermediaries reduce this uncertainty for both parties.

We will use these functions of reassortment/sorting, routinization, and searching in our construction of a technology-distribution function grid, or what we call the Internet Distribution Matrix.

What does technology do?

Understandably at this early stage, the focus has either been on the Web from a general marketing perspective, or as a marketing communication medium. While this attention is important and warranted, less attention has been given to the Web's impact on distribution channels, and this may turn out to be even more significant than its impact on communication. Indeed, as we shall argue, distribution may in the future change from channels to media. We discern three major effects that electronic commerce will have on distribution. It will kill distance, homogenize time, and make location irrelevant. These effects are now discussed briefly.

The death of distance

In the mid-1960s, an Australian named Geoffrey Blainey wrote a classic study of the impact of geographic isolation on his homeland. He argued that Australia (and, of course, neighbors such as New Zealand) would find it far more difficult to succeed in terms of international trade because of the vast physical distances between the country and world markets. Very recently, Frances Cairncross chose to satirize Blainey's title, *The Tyranny of Distance*, by calling her work on the convergence of three technologies (telephone, television, and computer), *The Death of Distance*. She contends that "distance will no longer determine the cost of communicating electronically." For the distribution of many products—those that can be digitized, such as pictures, video, sound, and words—distance will thus have no effect on costs. The same is true for services. For all products, distance will have substantially less effect on distribution costs.

Probing public records

Providing on-line access to public records via its KnowX Web site attracted a completely different market than Information America expected. Instead of small law firms and businesses seeking a cheap form of access to KnowX's databases of court decisions and legal documents, the site attracted everyday people who use the service to locate people, check real estate records, investigate lawsuits, and so forth.

KnowX had planned to generate revenue through the sale of the information from these databases (the records cost between 95 cents and $6.95, 86 euro cents to €6.32). However, small firms did not avail themselves of this service. To take advantage of the market of *little people*, KnowX shifted its strategy to charging 50 cents to $1 (45 to 90 euro cents) for searches during the period 11 a.m. through 6 p.m. (free the rest of the day). These searches now number between 6,000 and 7,000 per day.

Information America is responsible for the massive task of building and maintaining the records in the database. Although states and municipalities are starting to provide free on-line access to their public information, KnowX is the only site to provide a single source to public records.

Adapted from Gardner, E. 1999. Public records served Web-style. *Internet World*, Jan. 18, 11-12.

The homogenization of time

In the physical market, time and season predominate trading, and therefore by definition, distribution. We see evidence of this in the form of opening hours; activities that occur by time of day and in social and climatic seasonality. The virtual marketplace is atemporal; a Web site is always open. The seller doesn't need to be awake to serve the buyer and, indeed, the buyer does not have to be awake, or even physically present, to be served by the seller. The Web is independent of season, and it can even be argued that these media create seasonality (such as a Thanksgiving Web browser). Time can thus be homogenized—made uniformly consistent for all buyers and all sellers. Time and distance vanish, and action and response are simultaneous.

The irrelevance of location

Any screen-based activity can be operated anywhere on earth. The Web bookstore Amazon.com, one of the most written about of the new Web-based firms, supplies books to customers who can be located anywhere, from book suppliers who can be located anywhere. The location of Amazon.com matters to neither book buyers nor book publishers. No longer will location be key to most business decisions. We have moved from marketplace to *marketspace*. To compare marketspace-based firms to their traditional marketplace-based alternatives, one needs to contrast three issues: content (what the buyer purchases), context (the circumstances in which the purchase occurs), and infrastructure (simply what the firm needs in order to do business).

The best way to understand a firm like Amazon.com as a marketspace firm is to simply compare it to a conventional bookstore on the three criteria of content, context, and infrastructure. Conventional bookstores sell books; Amazon.com sells information about books. It offers a vast selection and a delivery system. The interface in a conventional bookstore situation is in a shop with books on the shelves; in the case of Amazon.com, it is through a screen. Conventional bookstores require a shop with shelves, people to serve, a convenient location, and most of all, large stocks of books; Amazon.com requires a fast efficient server and a great database. Try as they might, conventional bookstores can never stock all the books in print; Amazon.com stocks no, or very few, books, but paradoxically, it stocks them all. It really matters where a conventional bookstore is located (convenient location, high traffic, pleasant surroundings); Amazon.com's location is immaterial. Technology is creating many marketspace firms. In doing so, cynics may observe that it is enacting three new rules of retailing: *Location is irrelevant, irrelevant, irrelevant.*

The Internet distribution matrix

Contrasting the three effects of technology vertically, with the three basic functions of distribution channels horizontally, permits the construction of a three-by-three grid, which we call the **Internet distribution matrix**. This is shown in Figure 6-1. We suggest that it can be a powerful tool for managers who wish to identify opportunities for using the Internet and the Web to improve or change distribution strategy. It can also assist in the identification of competitive threats by allowing managers to concentrate on areas where competitors might use technology to perform distribution functions more effectively. Frequently, competition may not be from acknowledged, existing competitors, but from upstarts and from players in entirely different industries.

	Reassortment and sorting	Routinization	Searching
The death of distance			
The homogenization of time			
The irrelevance of location			

Figure 6-1. The Internet distribution matrix

Each cell in the matrix in Figure 6-1 permits the identification of an effect of technology on a distribution function. So, for example, the manager is able to ask what effect the death of distance will have on the function of reassortment and sorting, or what effect the irrelevance of location will have on the activity of searching, in his or her firm. In order to stimulate thought in this regard, and to aid vicarious learning, we now offer a number of examples of organizations using their Web sites to exploit the effects of technology on distribution functions. It should be pointed out that neither the technological effects nor the distribution functions are entirely discrete—that is, uniquely identifiable in and of themselves. In other words, it is not possible to say that a particular Web site is only about the death of distance and not about time homogenization, or location irrelevance. Nor is it possible to say that, just because a Web site changes reassortment and sorting, it does not affect routinization and searching. Like most complex organizational phenomena, the forces all interact with each other in reality, and so we have at best succeeded, hopefully, in identifying cases that illustrate interesting best practices, or a good example, in each instance.

The effects of technology on distribution channels

In this section, we move through the cells in the Internet distribution matrix and, in order of sequence, present cases of firms using their Web sites to exploit the effects of technology in changing distribution functions.

The death of distance and reassortment and sorting

Music Maker is a Web site that allows customers anywhere to create CDs of their own by sorting through vast lists of recordings by various artists of every genre. The Web site charges per song, and then allows the customer to also personalize the CD by designing, coloring, and labeling it. The company then presses the CD and delivers it to the customer. Rather than compile a collection of music for the average customer, like a traditional recording company, or attempting to carry an acceptable inventory, like a good conventional record store, Music Maker lets customers do reassortment and sorting for themselves, regardless of how far away they may be from the firm in terms of distance. If a customer wants Beethoven's "Fifth" and Guns'N'Roses on the same CD, they can have it. At present, distance is only a problem for delivery, and not for reassortment/sorting; however, in the not-too-distant future, even this will not be an impediment. As the costs of digital storage continue to plummet, and as transmission rates increase, customers may simply download the performances they like, rather than have a CD delivered physically, and then press their own CD, or simply store the sound on their hard drive.

The death of distance and routinization

A problem frequently encountered by business-to-business marketers with large product ranges is that of routinely updating their catalogs. This is required in order to accurately reflect the availability of new products and features, changes and modifications to existing products, and of course, price changes. Once the changes have been made, the catalog then needs to be printed, and physically delivered to customers who may be geographically distant, with all the inconvenience and cost that this type of activity incurs. The problem is compounded, of course, by a need for frequent update, product complexity, and the potentially large number of geographically dispersed customers.

DuPont Lubricants markets a large range of lubricants for special applications to customers in many parts of the world. Its catalog has always been subject to change with regard to new products, new applications of existing products, changes to specifications, and price changes. Similarly, GE Plastics, a division of General Electric, offers a large range of plastics with applications in many fields, and the company faced similar problems. Both firms now use virtual routinization by way of their Web sites to replace the physical routinization that updating of printed catalogs required previously. This can be done for customers regardless of distance, and the virtual catalog is, in a real sense, delivered instantaneously. Users are availed of the latest new product descriptions and specifications, and prices, and are also able to search the catalog for the best lubricant or plastic application for a particular job, whichever the case may be.

The death of distance and searching

Anyone who has experienced being a traveler in country A, who wants to purchase an airline ticket to travel from country B to country C, will know the frustration of being at the mercy of travel agents and airlines, both in the home country and also in the other two. Prices of such tickets verged on the extortionate, and the customer was virtually powerless as he or she tried to deal with parties in foreign countries at a distance, unable to shop on the ground (locally) and make the best deal. The German airline Lufthansa's global reservation system lets travelers book fares from anywhere in the world, to and from anywhere in the world, and permits them to pick up the tickets at the airport. Unlike the Web sites of many airlines, which tend to be dedicated, Lufthansa's allows the customer to access the timetables, fares, and routes of its competitors. In this way, distance no longer presents an obstacle to customers in their search for need satisfaction, because Lufthansa is able to directly interact with customers all over the world.

The homogenization of time and reassortment/sorting

In a conventional setting, students who wish to complete a degree need to be in class to take the courses they want, and so do the faculty who will present, and the other students who will take, the courses, all at the same time. Where two desired courses clash directly with regard to time slots, or are presented close together at opposite ends of the campus or on different campuses, the student is generally not able to take more than one course at a particular time. This problem is particularly prevalent for many MBA programs with regard to elective courses, and students have to choose among appealing offerings in a way that generally results in satisficing rather than optimizing. Traditional distance learning programs have attempted to overcome these problems but have only been partially successful, for the student misses the live interaction that real-time classes provide. The Global MBA (GEMBA) program of Duke University, Fuqua School of Business, allows its students to take the elective course lectures anywhere, anytime, over the Internet, and uses the medium to permit students to interact with faculty and fellow students. As the on-line brochure states, "Thanks to a unique format that combines multiple international program sites with advanced interactive technologies, GEMBA students can work and live anywhere in the world while participating in the program." Students enroll for the course from many different parts of the world and in many time zones, yet are now able to self-assort the MBA program that they really want.

The homogenization of time and routinization

Every two months, British Airways mails personalized information to the many millions of members of its frequent flyer Executive Club. The problem is that this information is out-of-date on arrival. When club members wish to redeem miles for free travel, they either have to call the membership desk at the airline to determine the number of available miles, or, more commonly, request a travel agent to do so for them. There is also the problem of determining how far the member can travel on the miles available.

Nowadays, members are availed of on-line, up-to-the minute, and immediate information on their status on the British Airways Web site. By entering a frequent flyer number and a security code, a member is able to get a report on available miles, and check on the latest transactions that have resulted in the earning of miles. Then, the member is presented with a color map of the globe with the city of preferred departure at the center. Other cities to which the member would be able to fly on the available miles are also highlighted. The member is also able do *what-if* querying of the site by increasing the number of passengers, or upgrading the class of travel. Time is homogenized, and transactions routinized, because members can perform these activities when it suits them, and not have to wait for a mailed report, or for the travel agent's office to open. What would be a highly customized activity (determining where the member could fly to and how) when performed by humans is reduced to a routine by a system.

The homogenization of time and searching

In many markets, the need to reduce uncertainty by searching is compounded by the problem that buyer and seller operate in different time zones or at different hours of the day or week. Even simple activities, such as routine communication between the parties, become problematic. Employee recruitment presents a good example of these issues—companies search for employees and individuals search for jobs. Both parties in many situations rely on recruitment agencies to enter the channel as intermediaries, not only to simplify their search processes, but also to manage their time (such as, when will it suit the employer to interview, and the employee to be interviewed?).

A number of enterprising sites for recruitment have been set up on the Web. One of these, Monster Board, lists around 50,000 jobs from more than 4,000 companies, including blue-chip employers rated among the best. It keeps potential employees informed by providing customized e-mail updates for job seekers and, of course, potential employers are able to access résumés of suitable candidates on-line, anytime.

The recruitment market also provides excellent examples of getting it wrong and getting it right on the Web as a distribution medium. For many years, the *Times Higher Education Supplement* has offered the greatest market for jobs in higher education in the United Kingdom and the British Commonwealth. Almost all senior, and many lower level, positions in universities and tertiary institutions are advertised in the *Times Higher*. In 1996, the *Times Higher* set up a Web site where job seekers could conveniently browse and sort through all the available positions. This must have affected sales of the *Times Higher*, for within a short while, the *Times Higher* Web site began to require registration and subscription, perhaps in an attempt to shore up revenues affected by a decline in circulation. Charging, and knowing what to charge for and how, on the Web are issues with which most managers are still grappling. Surfers, perhaps enamored of the fact that most Internet content is free, seem unwilling to pay for information unless it produces real, tangible, immediate, and direct benefits.

Universities in the United Kingdom may have begun to sense that their recruiting was less effective, or someone may have had a bright idea. At the same time as the *Times Higher* was attempting to charge surfers for access to its jobs pages, a consortium of universities set up a Web site called jobs.ac.uk, to which they all post available positions. Not only is the job seeker able to specify and search by criteria, but once a potential position is found, he or she is able to link directly to the Web site of the institution for further information on issues such as the student body, research, facilities, and faculty—or whatever else the institution has placed on its site. Jobs.ac.uk does not need to be run at a profit, as does the *Times Higher*. The benefits to the advertising institutions come in the form of reduced job advertising costs and being on a site where job seekers will obviously come to look for positions. This is similar to the way that shoppers reduce their search in the real world by shopping in malls where there is more than one store of the type they intend to patronize.

In traditional markets, where searching requires a physical presence, both buyer and seller need to interact at a mutually suitable time. Of course, this time is not necessarily suitable to the parties in a real sense, and is typically the result of a compromise.

Those who wish to transport large quantities of goods by sea either need to wait until a shipper in another country opens the office before placing a telephone call, or communicate by facsimile and wait for an answer. But what if capacity could be ascertained, and then reserved automatically? And, what if a shipper had spare capacity and wished to sell it urgently? SeaNet is a network that serves the global maritime industry 24 hours a day, regardless of time zones, by facilitating search for buyers and sellers. Reports indicate that this award-winning site is cash positive within a year, and that it experiences subscription renewals at a rate of 90 percent. Shippers can post their open positions, orders, sales, and purchase information onto the site. This information is updated almost instantly and can be accessed by any shipping company anywhere in the world searching the Internet in order to do business—not just subscribers. Companies that want to do business can then contact the seller by e-mail, or by more conventional methods. With the help of SeaNet's site, shippers can find the information they need quickly and easily.

The irrelevance of location and reassortment/sorting

Conventional computer stores attempt to serve the average customer by offering a range of standard products from computer manufacturers. Manufacturers rely on these intermediaries to inform them about what the typical customer requires, and then produce an average product for this market. Customers travel to the store that is physically near enough to them in order to purchase the product. In this market, location matters. The store must be accessible to customers and, of course, be large enough to carry a reasonable range of goods, as well as provide access and parking to customers.

Dell Computer is one of the real success stories of electronic commerce, with estimates of daily sales off its Web site needing to be updated on a daily basis, and at the time of writing, estimated to be in excess of $6 million (€5.5 million) each day. The company has been a sterling performer through the latter half of the 1990s, and much of this recent achievement has been attributed to its trading over the Internet. Using Dell's Web site, a customer is able to customize a personal computer by specifying (clicking on a range of options) such attributes as processor speed, RAM size, hard drive, CD ROM, and modem type and speed. A handy calculator instantly updates customers on the cost of what they are specifying, so that they can then adjust their budgets accordingly. Once satisfied with a specified package, the customer can place the order and pay on-line. Only then does Dell commence work on the machine, which is delivered to the customer just over a week later. Even more importantly, Dell only places orders for items such as monitors from Sony, or hard drives from Seagate, once the customer's order is confirmed. The PC industry leader Compaq's current rate of stock turnover is 12 times per year; Dell's is 30. This may merely seem like attractive accounting performance until one realizes the tremendous strategic advantage it gives Dell. When Intel launches a new, faster processor, Compaq effectively has to sell six-week-old stock before it is able to launch machines with the new chip. Dell only has to sell ten days' worth. Dell's location is irrelevant to customers—the company is where customers want it to be. Dell actually gets the customers to do some work for the company by getting them to do the reassortment and sorting themselves.

The irrelevance of location and routinization

Location has typically been important to the establishment of routines, efforts to standardize, and automation. It is easier and less costly for major buyers to set up purchasing procedures with suppliers who are nearby, if not local, particularly when the purchasing process requires lengthy face-to-face negotiation over issues such as price, quality, and specification. Recent examples of major business-to-business purchasing off Web sites, however, have tended to negate this conventional wisdom.

Caterpillar made its first attempt at serious on-line purchasing on 24 June 1997, when it invited preapproved suppliers to bid on a $2.4 million (€2.2 million) order for hydraulic fittings—simple plastic parts which cost less than a dollar but which can bring a $2 million (€1.8 million) bulldozer to a standstill when they go wrong. Twenty-three suppliers elected to make bids in an on-line process on Caterpillar's Web site. The first bids came in high, but by lunchtime only nine were still left revising offers. By the time the session closed at the end of the day, the low bid was 22 cents (20 euro cents). The previous low price paid on the component by Caterpillar had been 30 cents (27 euro cents). Caterpillar now attains an average saving of 6 percent through its Web site supplier bidding system.

General Electric was one of the first major firms to exploit the Web's potential in purchasing. In 1996, the firm purchased $1 billion (€910 million) worth of goods from 1,400 suppliers over the Internet. As a result, the company reports that the bidding process has been cut from 21 days to 10, and that the cost of goods has declined between 5 and 20 percent. Previously, GE had no foreign suppliers. Now, 15 percent of the company's suppliers are from outside North America. The company also now encourages suppliers to put their Web pages on GE's site, and this has been found to effectively attract other business.

The irrelevance of location and searching

Location has in the past been critical to the function of search. Most buyers patronize proximal suppliers because the costs of searching further afield generally outweigh the benefits of a possible lower price. This also creates opportunities for intermediaries to enter the channel. They serve local markets by searching for suppliers on their behalf, while at the same time serving producers by giving them access to more distant and disparate markets. Travel agents and insurance brokers are typical examples of this phenomenon. They search for suitable offerings for customers from a large range of potential suppliers, while at the same time finding customers for these suppliers that the latter would not have been able to reach directly in an economical fashion. The intermediary *owns* the customer as a result in these situations, and as a result, commands the power in the channel. Interactive marketing enables suppliers to win back power from the channel by interacting directly with the customer, thus learning more about the customer.

The U.K. insurance company Eagle Star now allows customers to obtain quotes on auto insurance directly off its Web site. It offers a 15 percent discount on purchase, and allows credit card payment. The company reports selling 200 policies per month in the first three months of this operation, generating $290,000 (€265,000) in premiums, and making 40,000 quotations. While it could be argued that these numbers are minuscule compared to the broker market, it should be remembered that this type of distribution is still in its infancy. Customers may prefer dealing directly with the company, regardless of its or their location, and in doing so, create opportunities for the company to interact with them even further.

Some long-term effects

The long-term effects of the death of distance, homogenization of time, and the irrelevance of location, on the evolution of distribution channels will be manifold and complex to contemplate. However, we comment here on three effects which are already becoming apparent, and which will undoubtedly affect distribution, as we know it in profound ways.

First, we may in the future talk of **distribution media** rather than distribution channels in the case of most services and many products. A medium can variously be defined as: something, such as an intermediate course of action, that occupies a position or represents a condition midway between extremes; an agency by which something is accomplished, conveyed, or transferred; or a surrounding environment in which something functions and thrives.

Traditionally, distribution channels have been conduits for moving products and services. The effects of the three technological phenomena discussed above will be to move distribution from channels to media. Increasingly in the future, distribution will be through a medium rather than a channel.

The key distinction that we make between a channel and a medium in this context concerns the notion of interactivity. Electronic media such as the Internet are potentially intrinsically interactive. Thus, whereas channels were typically conduits for products, an electronic medium such as the Internet has the potential to go beyond simply passive distribution of products and services, to be an active (and central) creative element in the production of the product or service. From virtual markets (e.g., Priceline.com) through virtual communities (e.g., Firefly) to virtual worlds (e.g., The Palace), the hypermedia of the Web actively constitutes respectively a market, a community, and a virtual world. The medium is thus the central element that allows consumers to co-create a market in the case of Priceline, their own service and produce in the case of Firefly, and their virtual world in the case of ThePalace. Critically, in each instance, the primary relationship is not between customers, but with the mediated environment with which they mutually interact. In summary, McLuhan's well-known adage that the "medium is the message" can be complemented in the case of interactive electronic medium such as the Web with the addendum that, in some cases, the *"medium is the product."*

A second effect of these forces on channel functions may be a rise in commoditization as channels have a diminished effect on the marketer's ability to differentiate a product or service. **Commoditization** can be seen as a process by which the complex and the difficult become simple and easy—so simple that anyone can do them, and does. Commoditization may easily be a natural outcome of competition and technological advance, which may see prices plunge and essential differences vanish. Commoditization will be accelerated by the evolution of distribution media that will speed information flow and thus make markets more efficient. The only antidote to commoditization will be to identify a niche market too small to be attractive to others, innovation sufficiently rapid to stay ahead of the pack, or a monopoly. No one needs reminding that the last option is even more difficult to establish than the preceding two.

Marketplace—linking buyers and sellers in a specialized market

SciQuest is a Web site aimed at providing a centralized marketplace for buyers and sellers in the specialized market segment of scientific equipment. Scientists looking for a particular product can search this site rather than follow the usual practice of flipping through numerous catalogs. There are an estimated 3,500 specialty suppliers in this field with a turnover of $10 billion (€9.1 billion). SciQuest hopes that buyers will find that using this marketplace provides easy access to the desired product and also allows them to make comparisons between the various suppliers instead of looking up the individual Web sites.

$10.5 million (€9.5 million) has been contributed by venture capitalists for the development of systems to enable all the data from the suppliers' catalogs to be linked to the site. The data will be stored in a hierarchical format with 20 general areas and 1,500 subcategories. Maintaining the data will have to be a cooperative effort between SciQuest and the suppliers, and SciQuest is developing a set of tools for the suppliers to use.

Initial revenue has been generated through the sale of ads on the site. SciQuest has expanded its role (and presumably its revenue) into selling the products through directing the buyers' orders to the various suppliers. To help and encourage the smaller suppliers who may not be used to taking orders from the Internet, SciQuest is aiming to make the tools work with fax, e-mail, and EDI.

Adapted from Andrews, W. 1999. Playing the role of digital middleman in a niche market. *Internet World*, Feb. 8, 12-13.

Disintermediation (and also reintermediation) is the third effect that we discern. As networks connect everybody to everybody else, they increase the opportunities for shortcuts—so that when buyers can connect straight from the computer on their desk to the computer of an insurance company or an airline, insurance brokers and travel agents begin to look slow, inconvenient, and overpriced. In the marketing of products, as opposed to more intangible services, this is also being driven by cheap, convenient, and increasingly universal distribution networks such as FedEx and UPS. No longer does a consumer have to wait for a retailer to open, drive there, attempt to find a salesperson who is generally ill-informed, and then pay over the odds in order to purchase a product, assuming the retailer has the required item in stock.

Products and prices can be compared on the Web, and lots of information gleaned. If one supplier is out of stock or more expensive, there is no need to drive miles to a competitor. There are generally many competitors, and all are equidistant, a mere mouse click away. These phenomena will all lead to what has been termed disintermediation, a situation in which traditional intermediaries are squeezed out of channels. As networks turn increasingly mass market, there is a continuous contest of disintermediation (see also the disintermediation threat grid on page 7)

The Web also creates opportunities for **reintermediation**, where intermediaries may enter channels facilitated electronically. Where this occurs, it will be because they perform one of the three fundamental channel functions of reassortment and sorting, routinization, or searching more effectively than anyone else can. Thus, we are beginning to see new intermediaries set up sites which facilitate simple price search, such as the U.K.-based site Cheapflights, which enables a customer to search for the cheapest flight on a route, and more advanced sites (e.g., Priceline) which actually purchase the cheapest fare when customers state what price they are prepared to pay. In a world where new and unknown brands may have an uphill battle to establish themselves, there may be opportunities for sites set up as honest brokers, merely to validate brands and suppliers on Web sites. In these constant games of disintermediation and reintermediation, customer relationships will be the winners' prize.

Dealing effectively with distribution issues in the future will require an understanding of the new distribution media, and how the new model will differ from the old. Most extant distribution and communication models are based on centralization, where the investment is at the core and substantially (as shown in Figure 6-2), and considerably lower on the periphery.

In the new model which is shown in Figure 6-3, investment is everywhere, and everywhere quite low. Essentially all that is required is a computer and a telephone line, and anyone can enter the channel. This can be as supplier or customer. Intermediaries can also enter or exit the channel easily; however, their entry and continued existence will still depend on the extent to which they fulfill one or more of the basic functions of distribution. It will also depend on the effects that technology have on distribution in the markets they choose.

Conclusion

In this chapter, we have developed the Internet distribution matrix, and suggest that it can be used by existing firms and entrepreneurs to identify at least three things. First, how might the Internet and its multimedia platform, the Web, offer opportunities to perform the existing distribution functions of reassortment/sorting, routinization, and searching more efficiently and effectively. Cases of organizations using the medium to perform these activities, such as those that we have identified, can stimulate thinking. Second, the matrix can enable the identification of competitors poised to use the media to

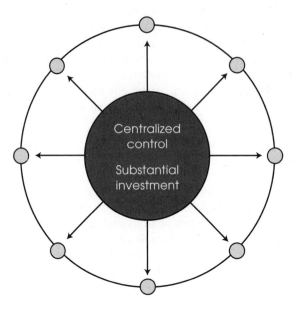

Figure 6-2. The mass model of distribution and communication

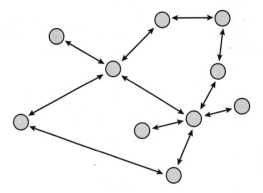

Figure 6-3. The network model of distribution and communication

change distribution in the industry and the market. Finally, the matrix may enable managers to brainstorm how an industry can be vulnerable. Neither the firm nor its immediate competitors may be contemplating using the Web to achieve radical change. However, that does not mean that a small startup is not doing so. And the problem with such small startups is that they will not operate in a visible way, or at the same time. In many cases, they might not even take an industry by storm, but they might very well deprive a market of its most valuable customers, as they exploit technology to change the basic functions of distribution.

Cases

Dutta, S., A. De Meyer, and S. Kunduri. 1998. *Auto-By-Tel and General Motors: David and Goliath.* Fontainebleau, France: INSEAD. ECCH 698-066-1.

Jelassi, T., and H. S. Lai. 1996. *CitiusNet: the emergence of a global electronic market.* Fontainebleau, France: INSEAD and EAMS. ECCH 696-009-1.

Subirana, B., and M. Zuidhof. 1996. *Readers Inn: virtual distribution on the Internet and the transformation of the publishing industry.* Barcelona, Spain: IESE. ECCH 196-026-1.

Additional readings

Blattberg, R. C., and J. Deighton. 1991. Interactive marketing: exploiting the age of addressability. *Sloan Management Review* 33 (1):5-14.

Cairncross, Frances. 1997. *The death of distance: how the communications revolution will change our lives.* London: Orion.

Hoffman, D. L., and T. P. Novak. 1996. Marketing in hypermedia computer-mediated environments: conceptual foundations. *Journal of Marketing* 60 (July):50-68.

Magretta, Joan. 1998. The power of virtual integration: an interview with Dell Computer's Michael Dell. *Harvard Business Review* 76 (2):73-84.

McKenna, Regis. 1997. *Real time: preparing for the age of the never satisfied customer.* Boston, MA: Harvard Business School Press.

Quelch, J. A., and L. R. Klein. 1996. The Internet and international marketing. *Sloan Management Review* 37 (3):60-75.

Stern, Louis W., and Adel I. El-Ansary. 1988. *Marketing channels.* 3rd ed. Englewood Cliffs, NJ: Prentice-Hall.

7

Service

Introduction

In many advanced economies, services now account for a far greater proportion of gross national product than manufactured goods (e.g., more than 75 percent of GDP and jobs in the U.S.). Yet, it is only in recent years that marketing academics, practitioners, and indeed, service firms have begun to give serious attention to the marketing of services, as distinct from products. It is generally thought that the marketing of services is more difficult, complex, and onerous because of the differences between services and products. The Web, we believe, will dramatically change forever this received wisdom. Most of the problems of services really don't matter on the Web. Services are no longer different in a difficult way. Using the Web to deliver services overcomes previously conceived limitations of services marketing, and in many cases, it creates hitherto undreamed of opportunities for services marketers.[1]

The Web offers marketers the ability to make available full-color virtual catalogues, provide on-screen order forms, offer on-line customer support, announce and even distribute certain products and services easily, and elicit customer feedback. The medium is unique because the customer generally has to find the marketer rather than vice versa, to a greater extent than is the case with most other media. In this chapter, we show how the Web is overcoming the traditional problems associated with the marketing of services. We are entering the era of *cyberservice*.

What makes services different?

What makes services different from products. In other words, what special characteristics do services possess? Services possess four distinct features not held by products, and an understanding of them is necessary to anticipate

---

1. An earlier version of this chapter appeared in Pitt, Leyland F., Pierre Berthon, and Richard T. Watson. 1999. Cyberservice: taming service marketing problems with the World Wide Web. *Business Horizons* 42 (1):11-18.

problems and to exploit the unique opportunities that some of these attributes provide. The unique characteristics of services are:

- **Intangibility:** Unlike products, services are intangible or impalpable, they cannot be seen, held, or touched. Whereas products are palpable things, services are performances or experiences. The main problem that intangibility creates for services marketers is that they have nothing to *show* the customer. Thus, experience and credence qualities are significantly important in the case of services.

- **Simultaneity:** In the case of goods, production and consumption are not simultaneous, and these activities do not occur at the same time or place. In the case of services, it is generally true that the producer and consumer both have to be present when a service is enacted.

- **Heterogeneity:** Products tend to possess a sameness, or homogeneity, that is not achieved by accident. Manufacturing lines produce homogenous products and have quality control procedures in place to test products as they come off the line, and to ensure that defective products don't reach the market. Services have the characteristic of heterogeneity. They vary in output, and mistakes happen in real time, in the customer's face, which creates a number of challenges for the services marketer.

- **Perishability:** Because services are produced and consumed simultaneously, they cannot be inventoried. For example, if there are twenty empty seats on an aircraft for a particular flight, the airline can't say, "Don't worry, stick them in a cupboard. We'll certainly be able to sell them over Thanksgiving." They are lost forever.

Cyberservice

Cyberservice overcomes many of the traditional problems of services marketing by giving the marketer undreamed of control over the previously capricious characteristics of services. This is because the Web, as an interactive medium, combines the best of mass production (based in the manufacture of products) and customization (typically found in custom-made services). The Web is the ultimate tool for mass customization. It has the ability to treat millions of customers as though they were unique. In this section, we illustrate how this is being done by innovative organizations using their Web sites to manage the difficulties previously caused by service characteristics.

Managing intangibility

1. Use the Web to provide evidence
Because customers can't see the service, we have to give them evidence of what it is they will get. This has long been a successful stratagem employed by

successful services marketers. McDonald's emphasizes its commitment to cleanliness not only by having clean restaurants, but by constantly cleaning. Cyberservice puts evidence management into overdrive. The Royal Automobile Club (RAC) enables users to enroll for membership on-line. Information provided on the site includes details of the benefits of RAC membership, the extent of assistance the club has provided, the service options available, and methods of payment. Most importantly, however, the site also e-mails a new member within a few minutes of him or her joining. This message confirms all details, and provides instantaneous, tangible proof of membership in the form of a membership number. Once the member notes this number, or better still, prints the e-mail message, it is as good as having a policy document. Under traditional service delivery systems, such as the mail, this would take a few days at least. While the member might have received confirmation over a telephone, the Web site provides instant tangible assurance.

One of Ford Motor Company's most innovative U.S. dealers is planning to install live video cameras in its service bays and relay a live feed to its Web site. Customers will be able to *visit* the service center and check the progress of their car's service. By opening up its service center for continuous customer inspection, the dealer is making very evident the quality of its service.

2. Use the Web site to tangibilize the intangible

Although services are considered intangible, effective Web sites can, and should, give services a tangible dimension. There is a simple, but critical, reason for this: when you can't really see what it is that you're buying, you look for clues, or what psychologists call cues. The prospective visitor to a Disney theme park is about to part with a not inconsiderable amount of money. No matter how much he or she has heard from friends and associates, until the visit actually occurs, the visitor will not be able to judge the quality of the experience. The Disney Web site tangibilizes a future dream. It provides graphic details on the parks themselves, allows children to see and listen to their favorite characters, examine the rides that they might take, and get further information, before booking the visit. It is well to remember, in general, that when managing Web sites, three critical elements stand out:

- **Quality of the Web site:** A site must have quality text, graphics, video, and sound. When the customer sees the Web site and not the firm, the Web site becomes the firm!

- **Frequency of update:** Surfers will generally not visit a site frequently unless it changes regularly. A Web site, no matter how engaging on first impression, will fail if it is not seen to change, refresh, and generally be perceived as up-to-date. Interpreted from the customer's perspective, it is almost the same as saying there is someone behind the Web site, who cares enough about it. Most importantly, there is someone who is concerned enough about the customer to constantly reinvigorate the Web site. The Web site is the firm's street front. Customer's expect it to change, just like the window displays of department stores.

- **Server speed:** In the pre-cyberservice days, service speed counted. In the Web environment, the surrogate for service speed is server speed and ease of navigation. Just as the customer won't wait endlessly in line for a bank teller, a fast food restaurant server, or a travel agent, they will not wait forever to access a slow Web site on a sluggish server. Customers will simply move on. Immediacy is central to service and a defining expectation in cyberspace.

3. Sampling in cyberspace

It is very difficult to sample a service. The best way to convince someone to purchase wine is to have them try a sample glass. If they like it, they may buy a case, or at least a bottle. Wine estates and fine wine stores realize this and use tastings as a major element of promotional strategy. Similarly, car dealers arrange demonstration drives, and bookstores have their wares on display for customers to browse through before making a choice. Sampling is far more difficult with services, because they are intangible. The Web has the potential to change all this.

Each year, Harvard Business School Publishing Services (HBSP) generates many millions of dollars worth of business selling case studies, multimedia programs, books, and of course, the famous *Harvard Business Review*. Previously, an instructor anywhere in the world wishing to examine a Harvard case study had to order a sample copy either by telephone, fax, or in writing, and then wait some days for the item to arrive, after having been physically dispatched by HBSP. Nowadays, approved instructors from all over the world browse the Harvard site, using powerful search facilities to find cases and other materials in which they are interested. When something relevant is found, the instructor downloads it in Adobe Acrobat format and prints it, complete with a watermark indicating that the case is a sample, not for further reproduction. The instructor can then decide whether to order the item. Similarly, the Web site also allows surfers to enroll for regular electronic updates on abstracts of new cases, articles, books, and other products that may be of interest. As well, visitors can subscribe to receive bimonthly the abstracts of articles in the latest *Harvard Business Review*.

4. Multiplying memories

Because services are intangible, the customer frequently relies on the testimony of others (word of mouth) to a greater extent than in the case of products. Whereas in the case of a product, the customer actually has something to show for it, with services there is usually just a memory.

Vivid Travel Network is a collection of Web sites based in San Francisco that links and integrates travel information resources from all over the world. The key feature of the service, in this context, is that it brings together people with experiences of different travel locations with people interested in visiting those locations. Those who have visited a location relive their vacation by writing about it, engaging in discussion and recollection with others who have also been there. At the same time, they provide valuable and highly credible word of mouth information to prospective visitors by allowing vast networks to multiply memories.

Managing simultaneity

Some of the features of simultaneity that the Web allows services marketers to manage include:

1. Customization

Because services are produced and consumed simultaneously, there is a possibility that the provider can customize the service. If this is done well, it can lead to giving the customer what he or she wants to a far greater extent than is the case with most products. The Web has the ability to excel at this, and because its capacity is based on information technology, data storage, and data processing, rather than employees and physical location, it can do it on a scale that traditional service providers would find impossible to match. Pointcast offers an individually customized news retrieval service. The customer selects categories of personal interest, such as news, sport, stock quotes, and weather. The service then scans news providers, and compiles a customized offering for each person, which is updated regularly either by the individual requesting additional items, or by the software learning what the individual likes and prefers, and searching for information that will satisfy these needs. Thus, no two individuals receive the same service from Pointcast.

2. Managing the customer as a part-time employee

In order to obtain services, the customer generally has to come inside the factory. Thus, in most conventional service situations, clients enter banks, vacationers go inside travel agencies, and university students attend classes in classrooms. Furthermore, once inside the service factory, the customer actually has to do a bit of work. Indeed, in the case of some services, a substantial amount of work. Not only does the customer come inside a service factory, and do some work, in many cases the quality of the service the customer receives is almost as dependent on the customer as it is on the efforts of the service provider. The customer can therefore be seen as a co-producer in service firms, and is, in a substantial sense, a part-time employee. In most service settings, this can be an opportunity to save costs and spark innovation.

The Web site of a well-known international service company illustrates how the medium can be used to manage profitably customers as part-time employees. The international courier company UPS allows customers access to its system through its Web site. The site reduces uncertainty by allowing customers to track shipments traveling through the system by entering the package receipt number. Furthermore, customers can request a pickup and find the nearest drop-off site. UPS still uses a large team of service agents and a major telephone switchboard to deal with customer inquiries. Now, however, millions of tracking requests are handled on-line each month. Many would have used the more expensive and time-consuming telephone system. Clearly, UPS gains considerable savings by switching customers from telephone to Web parcel tracking. Furthermore, customers prefer this form of service delivery, otherwise, they would not have adopted it with such alacrity.

3. Innovation as part of customer participation

If we understand that, in service settings, the customer is a necessary co-producer and participant in the service creation process, then we can become aware of many possible service innovations that can create advantage in competitive markets. If the customer is willing to do some work, we can create enjoyable environments for them to do it in, and we can also devise service efficiencies that lead to significant cost reductions.

Firefly is an example of using the customer's willingness to participate in the service production process to create service innovations on the Web. The Firefly network creates virtual communities of customers by getting them not only to give a lot of information about themselves, but also to do a lot of the work required to create this virtual community. Customers give information about their preferences regarding books, music, or films. Firefly then builds a profile of the customer's likes, which is continually updated as the customer keeps on providing more information—usually in the form of ratings on scales. Customers are also put in touch with others who have similar interests to their own. This information is then correlated with other customers' interests and enjoyment profiles to recommend new music, books, or films. Customers also give their opinions of the films, music, or books that they have seen, and this is then fed back to other customers. This information is not only very valuable to the customer, but a major asset to the company itself, which it can sell to film producers, record companies, or book sellers. Customer are thus not only co-creators of their own service and enjoyment, they also produce on behalf of Firefly a very valuable and saleable information asset.

4. Service industrialization

While service firms have to put up with the fact that the customer comes inside the factory, this is not always strictly true. It might be more appropriate to say that a fundamental dilemma facing services marketers is to decide on the extent to which they want the customer to come inside the factory.

It has been argued that service firms would more successful if they provided less service, not more! They should industrialize themselves, and become more like mass producers of goods than benevolent panderers to the whims of individuals. Rather than try to solve the problems that arise in service firms, they should try to eliminate them. Don't fix the system, change the system. In doing so, they will be giving the customers what they really want, not more service, but less service! To many marketers in general, and service marketers in particular, this might sound like heresy. However, a simple Web example allows us to illustrate vividly these points.

Consider how you would normally obtain a telephone number that you were unable to find. You would call directory inquiries, carefully enunciate the name, and what you know of the address of the desired party, wait while the operator found it (hopefully!), and then listen to a computer voice rapidly read the number. A Web site, Switchboard.com, is a giant national database that contains the names, telephone numbers, and addresses of more than 100 million households and a further million businesses in the U.S. Visitors simply type in a name to get a listing of all of the people in the country by that name. Further information that the visitor has, such as state, city, or street name, helps narrow the search considerably. The visitor is able to print and keep the listing, once found, and also use the Web site to automatically send a postcard to the person just tracked down. This is the Web site for which the length of visit is one of the longest—for once visitors realize its potential to find one number, they immediately see its value in being able to search for, and contact, long-lost family members, friends, and schoolmates. Yet, this unique service is entirely produced by machines.

The directory assistance example illustrates how redesigning the system to provide less service, by replacing the human element with a machine, actually provides more service. Customers now have access to more information, which is so often the core element of any service.

5. Reducing customer errors

When customers are part of the production process, their errors can directly affect the service outcome. Indeed, one-third of all customer complaints are related to problems caused by customers. Thus, ways must be found to make the consumer component, as well as the producer component, of services fail-safe. Customer errors arise during preparation for the encounter, the service encounter, or the resolution of the encounter. Some examples illustrate how cyberservice reduces or avoids customer errors in each of the stages.

Encounter preparation

Customers can be reminded of what they need to do prior to the encounter—what to bring, the steps to follow, which service to select, and where to go. Hampton Inn generates personalized driving instructions for travelers to get them from their starting location to the selected Hampton Inn at their destination. Travelers can select their type of route, direct or scenic.

The encounter

An advantage of cyberservice is that customers can be led precisely through a process repeatedly. For example, when buying books from Amazon.com the customer is stepped through the process of selecting books and providing payment and shipping details. No steps can be missed and the system checks the validity of entered information. Furthermore, customers don't type in book titles (a possible customer error); these are selected by clicking. Many Web sites require customers or prospects to enter their e-mail address twice because of the observed high customer data entry error rate. Of course, wherever possible, pull-down selection lists should be used so that customers have less opportunity to make errors.

Encounter resolution

On-line catalog companies, such as REI, e-mail customers a copy of their order so customers can correct any errors they may have made when entering delivery and order details.

The bills in the e-mail

Many companies are persuading their customers to use their Web-based billing systems rather than the traditional paper-based methods. MCI Worldwide Inc. plans to charge its corporate customers anywhere from $50 (€45) upwards for paper invoices which can be expensive, especially for large corporations whose bills can comprise reams of paper.

Although this would be the first time for a telecommunications company to charge for paper billing, MCI Worldwide is following a trend set by other industries to push customers towards the Web for some routine transactions because of the significant cost savings.

Interact, MCI's new Web-based billing and network monitoring system, is an MCI extranet accessed by customers using their Web browser and password. Corporate customers download the billing data, which they can then analyze by extension line, department, or time period.

Adapted from Hamblen, M. 1999. MCI pushing users toward Web billing. *Computerworld*, Jan. 25, 4.

Managing heterogeneity

Once more, there are a few things that the services marketer can manage on the Web in order to overcome the problems occasioned by service heterogeneity. Indeed, the Web offers unique opportunities in this regard.

1. Service standardization on the Web site

Some services marketers are reluctant to standardize service activities because they feel that this tends to mechanize and dehumanize an interaction between individuals. In some circumstances this is true, but that doesn't mean that managers shouldn't look for opportunities to produce service activities in as predictable and uniform a way as possible. Many people are cynical about the sincerity of the greeting, thanks, and farewell that one receives in a McDonald's restaurant. However, by standardizing something as simple as this, the company has ensured that everyone is greeted, thanked, and bid farewell, in a setting where real warmth and friendliness don't matter all that much anyway. McDonald's has succeeded in eliminating much of the unpredictability that customers still face in so many other similar restaurant settings, surliness or complete indifference, or alternatively, service which is gushingly insincere. The real skills of services marketers becomes apparent in their ability to decide what should be standardized, and what should not.

Security First Network Bank (SFNB), which was one of the first financial services institutions to offer full-service banking on the Internet, uses a graphic metaphor—a color picture of the lobby of a traditional bank—to communicate and interact with potential and existing customers. Whereas in a real bank the customer might encounter great or indifferent service, warmth or rudeness, competence or incompetence, depending on the individual who serves them, in SFNB, the service is relevant and highly consistent.

2. Electronic eavesdropping on customers' conversations

Firms must listen to different consumer groups to ensure that they are hearing what customers are saying and how they are perceived as responding to their complaints, concerns, and ideas. They need to listen to three types of customers: external customers, competitors' customers, and internal customers (employees).

Everyday on the Internet, customers are talking about products. Newgroups and listservs provide forums for consumers, throughout the world, to pass comment on a company's products and services. Furthermore, bad news travels at megabits per second to millions of customers, as Intel found when the flawed Pentium chip was detected. Companies can eavesdrop on these conversations and respond when appropriate. In addition, they can collect and analyze customers' words to learn more about their customers and those of their competitors. Internally, an organization can set up electronic bulletin boards to foster communication from internal customers.

Traditional focus groups meet same time and same place. Our early work with electronic focus groups indicates that the chains of time and space can be easily snapped. We have successfully operated electronic focus groups spanning seven time zones and three countries.

Cyberservice means listening to more customers more intently and reacting electronically in real-time. It also means everyone in the organization can listen to customers. Key insights can be broadcast on internal bulletin boards so that everyone understands what the customer truly wants. There has never been a better opportunity to get closer to customers and stay focused on their needs.

3. Service quality

Whereas good quality can be controlled into, and bad quality out of, the production process for goods, in the case of services this is made much more difficult by heterogeneity. Thus, service quality needs to be carefully managed. In order for it to be managed, of course, it needs to be measured. If you can't measure something, you can't manage it. In the last ten years, tremendous progress has been made in the measurement of service quality.

Interactive, Web-based questionnaires are a convenient and inexpensive way of collecting customers' perceptions of service quality or some other aspect of a service. Computing and IT services at the University of Michigan has an on-line survey for its customers to complete. An on-line version of SERVQUAL, a widely used measure of service quality, can capture customers' expectations and perceptions of service quality and e-mails these data to a market research company. The real pay-off of Web-based questionnaires is in reducing the length of the feedback loop so that service quality problems are rapidly detected and corrected before too many customers are disaffected.

Business-to-business auctions

By using FreeMarket On-line Inc.'s private on-line auction site, buyers in industrial markets are achieving savings of an average of 15 percent. FreeMarket helps buyers develop requests for proposals (RFPs), scouts potential suppliers, and then trains the suppliers in the bidding software. Suppliers participate in the on-line auction and have the opportunity to counterbid against other bids.

Small percentage savings in these multi-million industrial markets are significant, even with fees of $50,000 to $100,000 (€45,500 to €91,000) per month for auction and consulting services. At present, not all the major suppliers are participating in the on-line bidding, but FreeMarket believes their site will attract more suppliers as their business increases.

With the huge industrial markets, business-to-business auction sites have the capability of generating much greater revenues than the popular consumer auction sites.

Adapted from Machlis, S. 1998. Auction site woos corporate bidders. *Computerworld*, Dec. 7, 45-46.

Managing perishability

Because products are produced before they are consumed, many can be stored until needed. Services cannot, for they are produced and consumed simultaneously, as we know. This gives them the characteristic of perishability. Services cannot be inventoried. To understand and minimize the effects of service perishability, astute services marketers are using Web sites to manage two things, supply and demand.

1. Managing supply on the Web site

Managing supply in a conventional service setting requires controlling all those factors of service production which affect the customer's ability to acquire and use the service. Thus, it traditionally includes attention to such variables as opening and closing hours, staffing, and decisions as to how many customers will be able to use the service at any particular time. On the Web, these issues are circumvented, for the Web site gives the services marketer the ability to provide 24-hour service to customers anywhere. British Airways uses its Web site to provide services that, under conventional circumstances, would have been limited by people, time, and place. Customers are now able to purchase tickets off the Web site at any time convenient to them, without standing in line, from any place. British Airways provides a service to its Executive Club members whereby they regularly mail details on the frequent flyer program and miles available, as well as staffing a desk during office hours to which calls can be made. The human, time, location, and cost limitations of this are obvious.

2. Directing demand on the Web site

Services marketers also cope with service perishability by managing demand. That is, they use aspects of the services marketing mix, such as promotions, pricing, and service bundling, to stimulate or dampen demand for the service. Most service businesses are characterized by a high fixed cost component as a proportion of the total cost structure. Thus, in many situations, even very low prices for those last few seats or those last few rooms can be easily justified—20 or 30 percent of list price is still better than nothing when the service would have perished anyway. Many airlines are now conducting on-line ticket auctions on their Web sites as a way of managing demand. Airlines typically fill only two-thirds of their available capacity. By auctioning off unsold seats for imminent flights at low prices, the potential exists to approach 100 percent capacity. This is likely to result in substantial increases in airline profits, as full capacity on flights is reached with little or no increase in total costs.

Finally, some services marketers make good use of service bundling—putting together inclusive packages of services in a way that allows value to the customer to far exceed what he or she would have spent purchasing each component of the bundle individually. Microsoft's travel Web site,

Expedia.com, allows customers to shop for vacations, flights, car rentals, and tours and to combine these into personalized travel bundles, all from one location.

Conclusion

Services possess unique characteristics: intangibility, simultaneity, heterogeneity, and perishability. These have traditionally presented serious challenges to the services marketer. Cyberservice has the ability to ameliorate many of the problems traditionally associated with service, and even turn them into singular opportunities. Ironically, in the near future, it may be products that are more troublesome to marketers than services. The Web overturns the traditional hierarchy between products and services. How does cyberservice achieve this? The answer lies in three characteristics of cyberspace—the ability to quantize, search, and automate. Quantization of services (the breaking down of services into their smallest constituent elements) allows unparalleled mass customization (the recombination of elements into unique configurations). Search facilitates hyper-efficient information markets, matching supply and demand at a level previously unattainable. Automation allows service bottlenecks to be bypassed, returning power and choice to the customer, and overcomes the traditional limitations of time and space.

Cases

Charlet, J.-C., and E. Brynjolfsson. 1998. *BroadVision*. Graduate School of Business, Stanford University, OIT-21.

Huff, S. L. 1998. *Scantran*. London, Canada: University of Western Ontario. 997E010.

Charlet, J.-C., and E. Brynjolfsson. 1998. *Firefly Network (A)*. Graduate School of Business, Stanford University, OIT-22A.

References

Berry, L. L., and A. Parasuraman. 1997. Listening to the customer—the concept of a service-quality information system. *Sloan Management Review* 38 (3):65-76.

Chase, R. B., and D. M Stewart. 1994. Make your service fail-safe. *Sloan Management Review* 35 (3):35-44.

Levitt, T. 1976. The industrialization of service. *Harvard Business Review* 54 (5):63-74.

Zeithaml, V., A. Parasuraman, and L. L. Berry. 1990. *Delivering quality service: balancing customer perceptions and expectations*. New York, NY: Free Press.

8 Pricing

Introduction

Uniquely among the marketing mix variables, price directly affects the firm's revenue. Thus, the setting of prices is a critical issue facing managers. Traditional economic theory argues that decision-makers are rational, and that managers will set prices to maximize the firm's surplus. Consumers are similarly rational and will seek to maximize their surplus by purchasing more of a product or service at lower prices than they will when prices are higher. Prices in markets that approach a form of pure competition are set by a confluence of supply and demand, and firms attempt to price goods and services so that marginal revenues equal marginal costs. Yet, in the real world of marketing, there is ample evidence of the bounded rationality of marketing decision-makers who seem to set prices with things other than profit maximization in mind. Pricing strategy sometimes focuses on market share objectives, while at other times it concentrates on competitors by either seeking to cooperate with or destroy them. Frequently, pricing is about brand or product image, as marketers seek to enhance the status of a brand by concentrating on its position in the mind of the customer, rather than on volume. Likewise, customers are in reality as emotional as they are rational, and purchase brands for the status and experiences that they confer, rather than merely on the utility that they provide.

From a marketing perspective, managers have tended to employ a range of pricing strategies to attain various organizational objectives. Most marketing textbooks describe the pricing of new products as high on launch and then the lowering of these prices at a later stage in order to *skim the cream* off the market. Or, firms attach low prices to new products right from the beginning of the life cycle, in order to ward off competition and *penetrate* the market. Managers have also resorted to pricing tactics such as discounting and rebates, price bundling, and psychological or *odd-number* pricing in order to appeal to customers. While theory suggests that customers are rational, the reality of most markets has meant that this rationality is bounded by such issues as product and information availability, the cost of search, and the inability of small customers to dictate price in any way to large suppliers. The advent of a new medium will change—is in fact already changing—the issue of price for both suppliers and customers in a way that is unprecedented. While the Internet, and its multimedia platform, the Web, have been seen by most marketers to be primarily about promotion and marketing communication, the effects that they will have on pricing will in all likelihood be far more profound.

In this chapter, we explore the impact that the Web will have on both the pricing decisions that managers make, and the pricing experiences that customers will encounter. For comfortable marketers, the Web may have the most unsettling pricing implications they have yet encountered; for the adventurous, it will offer hitherto undreamed-of opportunities. For many customers, the Web will bring the freedom of the price-maker, rather than the previously entrenched servitude of the price-taker. We introduce a scheme for considering the forces that determine a customer's value to the firm, and the nature of exchange. We use this scheme to enable the identification of forces that will affect pricing on the Web, and then suggest strategies that managers can exploit.

Click and clip—coupons on the Web

Consumers love to get a discount, and two sites offering discount coupons attracted more than 1.8 million unique visitors during December 1998. This popularity of on-line coupons continues to grow and the companies using these sites are finding they provide an efficient way of reaching potential consumers.

Coolsavings, Inc. has more than 1.3 million registered households with revenue increasing by a factor of 12 in a year. Its 60 national accounts include H&R Block Inc., Kmart Inc., and Kids "R" Us. H&R Block reported that redemption increased from around 2 percent with traditional paper coupons to over 10 percent with downloaded coupons.

The two coupon sites offered by Supermarkets Online Inc. received 645,000 unique hits in one week. One of the sites, Valuepage.com, offers a bar-coded shopping list for discounts at 9,000 participating supermarkets.

Costs of these methods need to be considered. Although the delivery costs through the Internet are less than via the newspaper or mail, the difference may be chewed up by the extra promotional costs of the Web.

Adapted from Machlis, S. 1999. Coupon clipping hits the Web—big time. *Computerworld*, Feb. 15, 44.

Web pricing and the dynamics of markets

For customers, the Web facilitates search. Search engines such as Excite, Yahoo!, and Lycos allow the surfer to seek products and services by brand from a multitude of Web sites all over the world. They are also able to hunt for information on solutions to problems from a profusion of sites, and access the opinions and experiences of their peers in different parts of the world by logging on to bulletin boards and chat rooms. The use of such agents has been touted to reduce buyers' search costs across standard on-line storefronts, specialized on-line retailers, and on-line megastores, and to transform a diverse set of offerings into an economically efficient market. The new promise of intelligent agents (pieces of software that will search, shop, and compare prices and features on a surfer's behalf) gives the Internet shopper further buying power and choice.

The search phase in the consumer decision-making process, which can be costly and time-consuming in the real world, is reduced in terms of both time and expense in the virtual. An abundance of choice leads to customer sophistication. Customers become smarter, and exercise this choice by shopping around, making price comparisons, and seeking greatest value in a more assertive way. Marketers attempt to deal with this by innovation, but this in turn leads to imitation by competitors. Imitation leads to more oversupply in markets, which further accelerates the cycle of competitive rationality by creating more consumer choice. The Web has the potential to accelerate this cycle of competition at a rate that is unprecedented in history, creating huge pricing freedoms for customers, and substantial pricing dilemmas for marketers.

There are two simple but powerful models that may enable us to gain greater insight into pricing strategies on the Web. We integrate these into a scheme that is illustrated graphically in Figure 8-1. The first of these simply applies the well-known Pareto-principle, also known as the 80-20 rule, to the customer base of any firm. For most organizations, all customers are not created *equal*—some are much more valuable than others. For example, one Mexican cellular phone company found that less than 10 percent of its customers accounted for around 90 percent of its sales, and that about 80 percent of customers accounted for less than 10 percent. Seen another way, while margins earned on the most valuable customers allowed the Mexican company to recoup its investment in them in a matter of months, low-value customers took more than six years to repay the firm's investment in them.

In the diagram in Figure 8-1, we have divided a firm's customer base into four groups, which may best be understood in terms of the frequent flyer schemes run by most airlines nowadays. By far the largest group numerically, the C category customers nevertheless account for a very small percentage of an airline's revenues and profits. These are probably customers who are not even members of the frequent flyer program, and if they are, they are likely to be *blue card* members who inevitably never accumulate enough air miles to be able to spend on anything. They are unlikely to be loyal customers; they don't fly often, and when they do, their main consideration is the ticket price. For the sake of a few dollars, euros, or yen, they will happily switch airlines and fly on less than convenient schedules. Category B customers are like the *silver card* frequent flyers of an airline. They fly more frequently than Cs, and may even accumulate enough miles or points to claim rewards. However, they are still likely to be price sensitive, and exhibit signs of promiscuity by shopping around for the cheapest fares. The A category customers represent great value to the firm—in airline terms these are *gold card* holders. They use the product or service very frequently, and are probably so loyal to the firm that they do not shop around for price, even when there may be significant differences between suppliers. Because they represent substantial value to a firm such as an airline, they may be rewarded not only with miles, but special treatment, such as upgrades, preferential seating, and the use of lounges. Finally, the A+ category of customers represents a very small, but very valuable, group who account for a disproportionately large contribution to revenues and profits. Not only do these customers reap the rewards of value and loyalty, they are probably known by name to the firm, which inevitably performs service beyond the normal for them. An unsubstantiated but persistent rumor has it that there is a small handful of British Airways customers for whom the airline will even delay the Concord!

The second model in Figure 8-1 is derived from Deighton and Grayson's (1995) notion of a spectrum of exchange based on the extent to which an exchange between actors is voluntary. Thus, at one extreme, exchange between actors can be seen as extremely involuntary, as in the case of theft by force. At least one party to this type of exchange does not wish to participate, but is forced to by the other's actions. At the other extreme, an example of an extremely voluntary form of exchange would be the trading of stocks or shares by two traders on a stock exchange trading floor. This type of exchange is *unambiguously fair*, with no need for inducement for either party to act. Here, both actors participate entirely voluntarily for mutual gain—neither is able to buy or sell *better* shares or stocks at a price. Indeed, economists would argue that this bilateral exchange is the closest approximation to pure competition in the microeconomic sense. The two fully informed parties believe that each will be better off after the exchange. The market is highly efficient if price itself contains all the information that the parties need to make their decisions. Market efficiency is the percentage of maximum total surplus extracted in a market. In competitive price theory, the predicted market efficiency is 100 percent where the trading maximizes all possible gains of buyers and sellers from the exchange.

Returning once more to the other end of the spectrum, the next least voluntary form of exchange between actors is theft by stealth, where one actor appropriates the possessions of the other without the other's knowledge. This

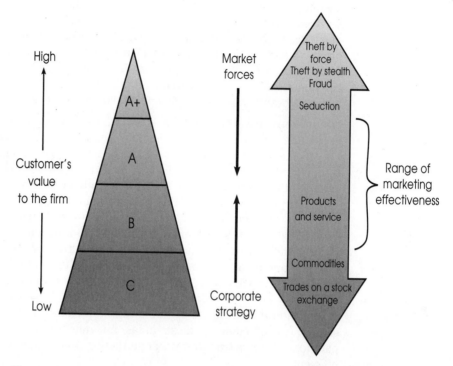

Figure 8-1. Customer value categories and exchange spectrum

follows on to the next point of fraud, where one party to the exchange enters into a transaction with the other in such a way that he or she is deliberately deceived, tricked, or cheated into giving up possessions without receiving the expected payment in return. Back on the other extreme of the spectrum, there are commodity exchanges, where actors buy and sell commodities such as gold, oil, copper, grain, and pork bellies. There is little or no difference between the product of one supplier and another—gold is gold is gold, commodities are commodities. The price of the commodity contains sufficient information for the parties to decide whether they will transact, and one seller's commodity is exactly the same as another's.

Between the extremes of the spectrum there is a gray area, which we label a **range of marketing effectiveness**. Adjacent to fraud there is what Deighton and Grayson refer to as *seduction,* which is an interaction between marketer and consumer that transforms the consumer's initial resistance to a course of action into willing, even avid, compliance. Seduction induces consumers to enjoy things they did not intend to enjoy, because the marketer entices the consumer to abandon one set of social agreements and collaborate in the forging of another.

Second, and next to commodities, there is the vast array of products and services purchased and consumed by customers. While the customer may in many cases be *seduced* into purchasing these, frequently some of these products and services bear many of the characteristics of commodities. In a differentiated market, products vary in terms of quality or cater to different consumer preferences, but frequently the only real differences between them may be a brand name, packaging, formulation, or the service attached to them.

Where does marketing, as we know it, work best along this spectrum of exchange? The answer is, in a narrow band, labeled the range of marketing effectiveness; straddling most products and services, and extending from somewhere near the middle of seduction, to somewhere near the near edge of commodities. Here, the parties are not equally informed. There is information asymmetry, and the merit of the transaction being more or less certain for one than the other. Marketing induces customers to exchange by selling, informing or making promises to them. Obviously, activities such as theft by force or stealth, and also fraud, cannot be seen as marketing. Yet, marketing is also unnecessary, or at best perfunctory, at the other end of the spectrum. Two traders on a stock exchange floor can hardly be said to market to each other when they trade bundles of stocks or shares. The price contains all the information the parties to the transaction need to do the deal. The market is simply too efficient in these areas for marketing to work well—almost paradoxically, it is true to say that marketing is not effective when markets are efficient.

Bringing the two concepts (the Pareto distribution of the customer base, and the exchange spectrum) together may help us understand pricing strategy more effectively, particularly with regard to the effect of the Web on pricing for both sellers and customers. The objective of firms, with regard to the Pareto distribution, should be to:

- migrate as many customers upward as possible. That is, to turn C customers into Bs, Bs into As, and so forth. By doing this, the firm will increase its customer equity, or in simple terms, maximize the value of its customer transaction base.

Forces in the market, however, including competition and the customer sophistication, tend to:

- force the customer distribution down, turning As to Bs, and Bs to Cs.

Similarly, in the case of the exchange spectrum, marketing's task is one of:

- moving products or services away from the zone of commodities, and more to the location of seduction.

Likewise the marketplace forces of competition and customer sophistication have the effect of:

- commoditization, a process by which the complex and the difficult become simple and easy—so simple and easy that anybody can do them, and does. Commoditization is a natural outcome of competition and technological advance, people learn better ways to make things and how to do so cheaper and faster. Prices plunge and essential differences vanish. Cheap PCs and mass-market consumer electronics are obvious examples of this.

It is thus incumbent upon managers to understand the forces that may impel markets towards a preponderance of C customers, and products and services towards commodities. Technology is manifesting itself in many such effects, and the Web is an incubator at present. On a more positive note, technology also offers managers some exciting tools with which to overcome the effects of market efficiency and with which to halt, or at least decelerate, the inevitable degradation of the customer base. These are the issues that are now addressed.

Flattening the pyramid and narrowing the scope of marketing

While firms attempt to migrate customers upward in terms of customer value, and to broaden the range of marketing effectiveness on the spectrum of exchange, there are forces at work in the market that mitigate in the opposite direction. While these forces occur naturally in most markets, the effect of information technology has been to put them into overdrive. These forces are now discussed.

Technology facilitates customer search

Information search by customers is a fundamental step in all models of consumer and industrial buying behavior. Search is not without sacrifice in terms of money, and especially, time. A number of new technologies are emerging on the Internet that greatly facilitate searching. These vary in terms of their ability to search effectively, and also with regard to what they achieve for the searcher. Of course, some are well along the road to full development and implementation, and others are still on drawing boards. The tools also range from a simple facilitation of search, through more advanced proactive seeking, to the actual negotiation of deals on the customer's behalf. However, all hold significant promise. These tools are described briefly in Table 8-1.

At the very least, tools in Table 8-1, such as search engines, directories, and comparison sites can reduce the customer's costs of finding potential suppliers, and those of making product and price comparisons. More significantly, the more sophisticated tools, such as true bots and agents, will seek out lowest prices and even conduct negotiations for lower prices.

Table 8-1: Tools that facilitate customer search

Type of tool	Functions	Examples
Search engine	Software that searches Web sites by key word(s).	AltaVista and Hotbot.
Directory	A Web site containing a hierarchically structured directory of Web sites.	Yahoo!
Comparison site	A Web site that enables comparisons of product/ service category by attributes and price.	CompareNet, a Web site that lists comparative product information and prices.
Shopbot	A program that shops the Web on the customer's behalf and locates the best price for the sought product.	Bots used by search engines Lycos and Excite.
Intelligent agent	A software agent that will seek out prices and features and negotiate on price for a purchase.	Kasbah, a bot being developed by MIT, can negotiate based on the price and time constraints provided.

Reduction of buyers' transaction costs

Nobel prize winner in economics, Ronald Coase, introduced the notion of transaction costs to the economics literature. Transaction costs are a set of inefficiencies that should be added to the price of a product or service in order to measure the performance of the market relative to the non-market behavior in firms. Of course, there are also transaction costs to buyers, including consumers. The different types of transaction costs, examples of these for customers, and how the Web may reduce them are illustrated in Table 8-2. Obviously, some of these transaction cost reductions are real and monetary; in other cases, they may be more psychic in nature—such as the relating of poor service over the Internet on bulletin boards as a form of customer revenge (and this in turn can reduce transaction costs for other customers).

Customers make, rather than take, prices

Particularly in consumer markets, suppliers tend to make prices while customers *take* them. A notable exception would be auctions, but the proportion of consumer goods purchased in this way has always been very small, and has been mainly devoted to used goods. There are a number of instances on the Web where the opposite situation is now occurring. On-line

Table 8-2: Transaction costs and the Web

Transaction costs	Examples of how the Web can affect
Search costs (finding buyers, sellers)	A collector of tin soldiers wishes to identify sources. He can use search engines and comparison sites, using the search term "tin soldier."
Information costs (learning)	A prospective customer wishes to learn more about digital cameras and what is available. Previously, she would have had to read magazines, talk to knowledgeable individuals, and visit stores. She can now access firm and product information easily and at no cost, obtain comparative product information, and access suppliers on the Web.
Bargaining costs (transacting, communicating, negotiating)	The time normally taken by a customer to negotiate can now be used for other purposes, as intelligent agents transact and negotiate on the customer's behalf. On-line bidding systems can achieve similar results. For example, GE in 1996 purchased $1 billion (€910 million) from 1,400 suppliers, and there is evidence of a substantial increase since. Significantly, the bidding process for the firm has been cut from 21 days to 10.
Decision costs	The cost of deciding over Supplier A vs. Supplier B, or Product A vs. Product B. The Web makes information available on suppliers (on their or comparative Web sites) and products and services. For example, Travel Web allows customers to compare hotels and destinations on-line.
Policing costs (monitoring cheating)	Previously, customers had to wait to receive statements and accounts, and then to check paper statements for correctness. On-line banking enables customers to check statements in real time. Chat lines frequently alert participants to good and bad buys, and potential product and supplier problems (e.g., the flaw in Intel's Pentium chip was communicated extensively over the Internet).
Enforcement costs (remedying)	When a problem exists with a supplier, how does the customer enforce contractual rights? In the non-Web world, this might require legal assistance. Publicizing the infringement of one's rights would be difficult and expensive. Chat lines and bulletin boards offer inexpensive revenge, if not monetary reimbursement!

auctions allow cybershoppers to bid on a vast range of products, and also services such as airline tickets, hotel room, and tickets. Already, many are finding bargains at the hundreds of on-line auction sites that have cropped up. Onsale.com is a huge auction Web site that runs seven live auctions a week, where people outbid one another for computer gear and electronics equipment. Onsale buys surplus or distressed goods from companies at fire sale prices so they can weather low bids.

At a higher level of customer price making, Priceline.com invites customers to name their price on products and services ranging from airline tickets to hotel rooms, and new cars to home mortgages. In the case of airline tickets, for example, customers name the price they are willing to pay for a ticket to a destination, and provide credit card details to establish good faith. Priceline then contacts airlines electronically to see if the fare can be obtained at the named price or lower, and undertakes to return to the customer within an hour. Priceline's margin is the differential between the customer's offer price and the fare charged by the airline.

Customers control transactions

Caterpillar uses its Web site to invite bids on parts from preapproved suppliers. Suppliers bid on-line over a specified period and a contract is awarded to the lowest bidder. Negotiation time is reduced and average savings on purchases are now 6 percent. In this way, the customer has taken almost total control of the transaction, for it has become difficult for suppliers to compete on anything but price. There is little opportunity to differentiate products, engage in personal selling, or to add service, as traditional marketing strategy would suggest suppliers do.

A return to one-on-one negotiation

In pre-mass market times, buyers and sellers negotiated individually over the sale of many items. It is possible that markets can move full circle, as buyers and sellers do battle in the electronic world. The struggle should result in prices that more closely reflect their true market value. We will see more one-on-one negotiation between buyers and sellers. As negotiation costs decrease significantly, it might be practical to have competitive bidding on a huge range of purchases, with a computer bidding against another computer on behalf of buyers and sellers.

Commoditization and efficient markets

The first goods to be bartered in electronic markets have been commodities. Price rather than product attributes, good selling, or warm advertising, is the determining factor in a sale. When the commodity happens to be perishable—such as airline seats, oranges, or electricity—the Web is even more compelling.

Suppliers have to get rid of their inventory fast or lose the sale. The problem on the Web is that when customers can easily compare prices and features, commoditization can also happen to some high-margin products. Strong brand names alone may not be enough to maintain premium prices. In many cases, branded products may even prove to be interchangeable. While customers may not trust a new credit card company that suddenly appears on the Web because they do not know its name, they may easily switch between Amex and Diners Club, or Visa and MasterCard.

Migrating up the pyramid and more effective marketing

It is possible that a marketer considering the forces discussed above may become pessimistic about the future of marketing strategy, especially concerning the flexibility of pricing possibilities. Yet, we contend that all is not doom and gloom, and that there are strategies which managers may exploit that will allow them to migrate customers up the Pareto pyramid, and which will make marketing more effective in a time of market efficiency. These strategies are now discussed.

Differentiated pricing all the time

The information age, and the advent of computer-controlled machine tools, lets consumers have it both ways: customized and cheap, automated and personal. This deindustrialization of consumer-driven economics has been termed mass customization. The Web has already been an outstanding vehicle for mass customization, with personalized news services such as CNN and Pointcast, personalized search engines such as My Yahoo!, and the highly customized customer interaction pages of on-line stores such as Amazon.com. However, the Web also gives marketers the opportunity to exploit a phenomenon that service providers such as airlines have long known, the same product or service can have different values to different customers. Airlines know that the Friday afternoon seat is more valuable to the business travelers, and charge them accordingly. The Web should allow the ultimate in price differentiation—by customizing the interaction with the customer, the price can also be differentiated to the ultimate extent, so that no two customers pay the same price.

Creating customer switching barriers

Technology allows sellers to collect detailed data about customers' buying habits, preferences, even spending limits, so they can tailor their products and prices to the individual buyer. Customers like this because it recognizes them as individuals and serves them better—recommends books that match their preferences, rather than some critic's; advises on music that matches their likes, rather than the top twenty; and puts them in touch with people or jobs that match them, rather than a list of names or an address list of employers. This, in turn, creates switching barriers for customers that competitors will find difficult to overcome by mere price alone. While the customer may be able to purchase the product or service at a lower price on another Web site, that site will not have taken the time or effort to learn about the customer, and so will not be able to serve the customer as well. In terms of economics, the customer will not actually be purchasing the same item.

Use technology to de-menu pricing

Most firms have resorted to *menu* or *list* pricing systems in the past to simplify the many problems that are caused by attempting to keep prices recorded and up-to-date. Pricing is not just about the Web—within firms, there can be private networks or extranets (see page 24), that link them with their suppliers and customers. Extranets make it possible to get a precise handle on inventory, costs, and demand at any given moment, and adjust prices instantly. Without automation, there is a significant cost associated with changing prices, known as the *menu cost*. For firms with large product or service lines, it used to take months for price adjustments to filter down to distributors, retailers, and salespeople. Streamlined networks reduce menu cost and time to near zero, so there is no longer a really good excuse for not changing prices when they need to be changed.

Be *much* better at differentiation: stage experiences

The more like a commodity a product or service becomes, the easier it is for customers to make price comparisons and to buy on price alone. Marketers have attempted to overcome this in the past by differentiating products by enhancing quality, adding features, and branding. When products reached a phase of parity, marketers entered the age of service, and differentiated on the basis of customer service. However, in an era of increasing service parity, it is the staging of customer experiences that may be the ultimate and enduring differentiator. The Web provides a great theater for the staging of unique personal experiences, whether esthetic, entertaining, educational, or escapist, and for which customers will be willing to pay.

Understand that customers may be willing to pay more

Marketers will make a big mistake by assuming that customers will expect and want to pay less on the Web than they do in conventional channels. Indeed, managers in many industries have a long record of assuming that customers underestimate the value of a product or service to them, and would typically pay less for it if given the chance. There is a very successful restaurant in London that invites customers to pay for a meal what they think it is worth. Some exploit the system and eat for free; however, on average, customers pay prices that give the establishment a handsome margin.

Consider total purchase cost

The purchase price is one element of the total cost of acquiring a product or service. Searching, shipping, and holding costs, for instance, can contribute substantially to the acquisition cost of some products. In those circumstances, where Web-based purchasing enables a customer to reduce the total cost of a purchase, that person may be willing to pay more than through a traditional channel. This argument can be formulated mathematically.

Let T = total acquisition cost,

P = purchase price,

O = other costs associated with purchase (including opportunity costs)

then $T = P + O$.

If we use w and t as subscripts to refer to Web and traditional purchases, then all things being equal, consumers will prefer to purchase via the Web when:
$$T_w < T_t.$$

Furthermore, consumers should be willing to pay a premium of $\delta = P_w - P_t$ where $\delta < O_t - O_w$.

For industrial buyers, opportunity costs may be a significant component of the total costs of a purchase. Also, particularly busy consumers will recognize the convenience of Web purchasing. Both of these groups are likely to be willing to pay a premium price for products purchased via the Web, if the result is a reduction in the total purchase cost. As a general pricing strategy, Web-based merchants should aim to reduce customers' O_t so they can raise P_w to just below the point where $T_w = T_t$.

The Web creates new ways for sellers to reduce the total costs that are faced by purchasers. Sellers can capitalize on these cost reductions by charging higher prices than those that are charged in traditional outlets.

Establish electronic exchanges

Many firms, particularly those in business-to-business markets, may find it more effective to barter rather than sell when prices are low. A number of electronic exchanges have already been successfully established to enable firms to barter excess supplies of components or products that would have otherwise been sold for really low prices. In this way, the firm rids itself of excess stock and receives value in exchange, in excess of the price that would have been realized. For example, Chicago-based FastParts Inc. and FairMarket Inc. in Woburn, Massachusetts, operate thriving exchanges where computer electronics companies swap excess parts.

Maximize revenue not price

Many managers overlook a basic economic opportunity. In many instances, it is better to maximize revenue rather than price. Airlines have perfected the science of yield management, concocting complicated pricing schemes that not only defy customer comparison, but that also permit revenue maximization on a flight, despite the fact that the average fare might be lower. Many airlines are now using Web sites to sell tickets on slow-to-fill or ready-to-leave flights, either on specials, or on ticket auctions. They also make use of external services, such as Priceline.com, wherein the customer, in a real sense, creates an *option* (the right, but not the obligation to sell a ticket), to both discern market conditions, and to sell last-minute capacity. Apart from their Web sites, airlines, hotels, and theaters can also use sites such as lastminute.com to market seats, rooms, and tickets a day or two before due date.

Reduce the buyer's risk

Every purchase incorporates an element of risk, and basic finance proclaims that risk and return are directly related. Thus, consumers may be willing to pay a higher price if they can lower the risk of their transaction.

Consider the case of auto dealers who can either buy a used car at an auto auction or purchase on-line via the Web. With on-line buying, it is possible for dealers to reduce their risk. Dealers can treat the on-line system as part of their inventory and sell cars off this virtual lot. The dealer can buy cars as needed to meet customer demand. In the best case scenario, a buyer requests a particular model, the dealer checks the Web site, puts a hold on a particular car, negotiates the price with the buyer, and then buys the car from the Web. In effect, the dealer sells the car before buying it. In this case, the dealer avoids the risks associated with buying a car in anticipation of finding a customer.

Dealers can be expected to pay a premium when the risk of the transaction is reduced. As Figure 8-2 illustrates, some dealers may perceive buying a car at an auction as higher risk, and thus expect a higher return compared to buying on-line. The difference in the return is the premium that a dealer will be willing to pay for a car purchased on-line, all other things being equal.

134

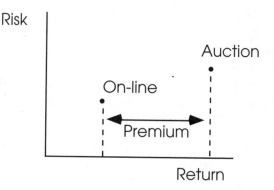

Figure 8-2. Risk and return trade-off

Web-based merchants who can reduce the buyer's risk should be able to command a higher price for their product. Typical methods for reducing risk include higher quality and more timely information, and reducing the length of the buy and resell cycle. This risk effect that we describe should be equally applicable to both organizational buyers and individual consumers. Again, the Web creates a special opportunity for sellers to reduce the risks that buyers face. In turn, sellers can charge a higher price to buyers for this benefit (risk reduction), which has been created on-line.

Conclusion

The Internet and the World Wide Web will have a fundamental influence on the pricing strategy of firms. Similarly, the technology will open many doors to buyers hitherto closed by the effects of time, cost, and effort. In this chapter, we have illustrated the effects of the new technology on price from two perspectives. First, the technology has the potential to change the shape and structure of the firm's customer base. At worst, it will flatten the customer base, turning the majority of a firm's customers into transactional traders who buy the spot. However, used wisely, it has the potential for migrating a significant number of a firm's customers up the value triangle, narrowing the customer base, and enabling the firm to build relationships with customers that negate the impact of mere price alone.

Second, the new media has the potential to move customers along the exchange spectrum in ways, and at rates, that have not hitherto been experienced. Technology may combine with market forces to reduce the vast majority of a firm's transactions to the level of commodity trades, leaving managers with little opportunity to make prices. A far more optimistic scenario, however, sees managers using the technology in combination with other marketing strategies to *seduce* the customer into a mutually valuable relationship. The chapter identifies the effects of technology and the forces in the market that have the potential to flatten and homogenize customer base triangles and shift customers disproportionately towards the commodity end of the exchange spectrum. The chapter also finds a number of approaches available to managers to put the brakes on these processes, and indeed, use the new technology to accelerate more effective pricing strategy.

Marketers have always viewed price as one of the instruments of policy in the marketing mix—a variable which, theoretically at least, can be manipulated and controlled according to circumstances in the business environment and the nature of the target market. In practice, however, many pricing decisions are not taken by marketers, and are based more on issues such as cost and competition than any notion of customer demand. Seen pessimistically, price decision making has been, and may continue to be, a mechanistic process of calculating costs and attempting markups, or a knee jerk reaction to market conditions and competitive behavior. A more optimistic view might be that pricing decisions can be as creative as those taken with regard to the development of new products and services, or the development of advertising campaigns. Indeed, pricing may be the last frontier for marketing creativity. Ignored or utilized mechanically, the Internet and the Web may be the vehicles that destroy the last vestiges of managerial pricing discretion. In the hands of the wise, these vehicles may be the digital wagons that carry pricing pioneers to the edge of the cyber frontier.

Cases

McKeown, P. G., and R. T. Watson. *Manheim Online*. Terry College, University of Georgia, Contact rwatson@uga.edu for a copy.

References

Bakos, J. Y. 1997. Reducing buyer search costs: implications for electronic marketplaces. *Management Science* 43 (12):1676-1692.

Cortese, A. E., and M. Stepanek. 1998. Good-bye to fixed pricing. *Business Week*, May 4, 71-84.

Deighton, J., and K. Grayson. 1995. Marketing and seduction: building exchange relationships by managing social consensus. *Journal of Consumer Research* 21 (4):660-676.

Desiraju, R., and S. M. Shugan. 1999. Strategic service pricing and yield management,. *Journal of Marketing* 63 (1):44-56.

Malone, T. W., J. Yates, and R. I. Benjamin. 1989. The logic of electronic markets. *Harvard Business Review* 67 (3):166-170.

Pine, B. J., B. Victor, and A. C. Boynton. 1993. Making mass customization work. *Harvard Business Review* 71 (5):108-119.

Pine, B. J., III, and J. H. Gilmore. 1998. Welcome to the experience economy. *Harvard Business Review* 76 (4):97-105.

9

Postmodernism and the Web: Societal effects

●●●●●●

Introduction

How are we to make sense of the Web and our involvement in it? This issue is no light matter, for how we make sense of what was, and is, delimits what will be. Thus, as more and more organizations establish a presence on the Web, the question of how to exploit the new medium presents challenges to practitioners and academics alike. How should economic and symbolic activity be conducted and conceptualized? How can we make sense of the new medium and our involvement in it? Different assumptions about this new medium will result in diverse activities—and the accompanying creation of different futures, and for businesses, varying degrees of marketing success or failure. This chapter explores the phenomenon of the Web using themes characterizing postmodernism, which is a collection of practices and thoughts that characterizes the information age. Postmodernism offers unique insights into information-rich contexts such as the Web.

Current media views and perspectives on the Web vary from dismissing it as a fad, to acclaiming it as the most significant contribution to communication since Gutenberg's invention of movable type. Trying to make sense of the Web is no simple matter, yet as an increasing number of organizations establish a presence in the medium, the need becomes pressing. Traditional models of business are unlikely to prove effective. While trends such as changing technology, commercialization, globalization, and demographics are important in understanding the Web, they represent only half the story.

More fundamental shifts can be uncovered by changing to a higher level of abstraction, by shifting from elements to relationships. Such has been the work of a divergent body of thinkers from artists to philosophers, historians to scientists, whose fragmented works have come to be known as postmodern. Indeed, postmodernism is seen as the label for thinking that resonates most strongly with the Information Age, just as modernism was the philosophy that embodied the Industrial Age. While there is little agreement on, or indeed collective understanding of, what constitutes postmodernism, various broad, overlapping themes are discernible.

●●●●●

In this chapter, we explore the Web through the postmodern themes of fragmentation, dedifferentiation, hyperreality, time and space, paradox, and anti-foundationalism. The first two themes—fragmentation (disintegration) and dedifferentiation—represent the opposites (or counterparts) of two of modernism's favorite systems concepts, integration and differentiation. The themes of hyperreality and space-time counter the traditional modernist assumption of what constitutes reality and progress. Anti-foundationalism, pastiche, and pluralism all question the modernist love of the one right answer (theory, way, view, voice, etc.). Although present in all media, we argue that it is the Web that most typifies postmodernist thought. This may be an important insight, for virtual realms (of which the Web is perhaps the most important), comprise perhaps the greatest marketing and organizational challenge and opportunity of the late twentieth century. Moreover, it was marketing practitioners who were among the first to embrace and explore the Web. Indeed, some argue that, after a technological medium, the Web is primarily a marketing medium.

What is modernism?

Modernity comprises those efforts to develop objective knowledge, absolute truths, universal morality and law, and autonomous art. It is the sustained attempt to free human thinking and action from the irrationality of superstition, myth, and religion. It comprises the basic summons toward human emancipation, clearly enunciated in the Enlightenment, a philosophical movement of the eighteenth century that emphasized the use of reason to bring about humanitarian reforms. Modernism has, at its heart, the idea of the rational person as the primary vehicle for progress and liberation. It stresses unity (underneath we are all the same) and progress (tomorrow will be better than today). So, to be modern is to find oneself in an environment that promises adventure, power, joy, growth, and transformation of ourselves and the world. Its themes, in contrast to postmodernism, comprise integration, differentiation, objective reality, linear time and delineated space, orthodoxy, unity, and foundationalism.

And postmodernism?

Modernism and postmodernism can be thought of as umbrella terms comprising many threads. However, modernism is a more coherent movement (because it values coherence) that has at its heart one fairly distinct core philosophy, ideology, and belief system. In contrast, postmodernism is characterized by multiple ideologies, multiple philosophies, and multiple beliefs. Indeed, postmodernism in some of its many guises actively seeks to undermine ideology and belief. Although nominally a late twentieth century movement, Postmodernism's intellectual roots can be traced back to Heraclitus, a fifth-century B.C. philosopher. The movement seeks to undermine and debunk the assumptions underpinning previous ages' thought systems and discourses. Obviously, this has the potential of degenerating into a rejection of everything.

The differences between modernism and postmodernism are summarized in Table 9-1. We explore these issues specifically in relation to the Web. The specific themes employed are fragmentation, dedifferentiation, hyperreality, time and space, paradox, and anti-foundationalism.

Table 9-1: Themes—modern and postmodern perspectives

Theme	Modernism	Postmodernism
Relationships between elements in a system	Integration and differentiation	Disintegration (fragmentation) and dedifferentiation
Reality	Reality is objective, "out there," discovered, and physical—"reality"	Reality is subjective, "in here," constructed, and imagined—"hyperreality"
Time and space	Linear, unitary, progressive chronology Space is delineated—space is time	Cyclic, multithreaded, fragmented chronology Space is imploded (negated)—time is space
Values	Orthodox, consistency, and homogeneity	Paradox, reflexivity, and pastiche
Attitude towards organizations and the social institutions that produce them	Foundationalism	Anti-foundationalism

Before commencing our exploration, a number of points should be made. First, there are aspects of the Web that are undeniably modern. Indeed, the Web can be viewed as the latest technological development of the modernist dream of adventure, progress, and liberation. However, it is our intention to focus on the Web's postmodern aspects. Second, ironically and yet relevant to a discussion of postmodernism, it is only the existence of a modern infrastructure (computers, integrated networks, and universal communication protocols) that enables a virtual and quintessentially postmodern world to be created. Finally, although the themes discussed are presented as distinct categories, this is for presentation purposes only. The categories are far from mutually exclusive— each contains, reflects, and refracts elements of the other.

Each theme is now discussed in turn under two sections. First, the theme is outlined in general abstract terms. Second, it is explored in specific relation to the Web.

Fragmentation

There is fragmentation or disintegration of traditional systems at all levels, including countries (the U.S.S.R. has broken up into many autonomous republics and the U.K. is devolving to give power to elected parliaments for Scotland and Wales), social groups (the family), political parties (the Communist party in many countries), and organizations (AT&T broke into three businesses in 1996). People's lives are becoming increasingly disjointed and fragmented in contemporary society.

Fragmentation and the Web

Fragmentation is apparent in a number of different spheres on the Web. First, the Web offers the ultimate in niche marketing: millions of discussion groups, newsgroups, special interest groups, and a greater diversity of products and services than any shopping or strip mall. Indeed, a significant amount of the material placed on the Internet is designed to reach a single person, a handful of people, or a group of less than 1,000.

Second, the very fact that people find companies' Web sites, rather than companies finding prospective customers, as in traditional media, means that the premise of mass marketing is rendered questionable at best, and irrelevant at worst. The advent of push technologies, though, may render part of the Web a little more familiar to traditional marketing. However, to bank on this is to misunderstand the nature of the Web and ignore its possibilities.

Third, people experience and behave differently in the new medium, with the Web resulting in a fragmentation of consensus. Research suggests that people feel more able to disagree and express differences in virtual media, and specifically on the Internet. Respondents in computer-mediated environments are more frank on sensitive topics, yet more inclined to offer false information in order to avoid identification. There is a lack of self-awareness and self-regulation of behavior. As well, the new medium has fueled and facilitated, to an unprecedented degree the fragmentation of the self. Individuals participating in MUDs, MOOs,[1] and discussion groups regularly adopt multiple, often-contradictory identities, personas, and personalities. For example, research reports that 20 percent of participants in these forums regularly pose as the opposite gender.

---

1. Multiuser dimension or dungeon (MUD), a multiple user electronic virtual world that is ongoing, comprising an electronically assembled group of people and bots, interacting in cyberspace. MOOs (MUDs-object oriented) are the more technologically sophisticated successors to MUDs.

Fourth, the Web is the ultimate global presence. This would seem to result in unprecedented unification and integration, yet the more closely we are linked, the more pronounced our differences become. Digitization breaks down wholes or entities (people, personalities, human beings) into millions of fragments, disconnected minutiae that can then be recombined across people into dehumanized profiles. This fragmentation mirrors the underlying Internet communication protocol, packet switching, which disassembles messages into packages (see page 20). These fragments, mingled with many other fragments, are transported from sender to receiver, where they are finally reassembled. The Web takes this digitization and packetizing to unprecedented lengths, with Internet companies, from banks to bookshops, typically knowing much more about their customers than traditional marketplace-based firms. Yet, paradoxically, as technology facilitates the much sought after one-to-one customer interaction, the customer becomes ever more fleeting, for the same technology allows customers to recreate and reinvent themselves in a collage of new co-existing images.

The Web fragments, and the successful Web companies of tomorrow, will exhibit this process—because their customers will.

Dedifferentiation

The dedifferentiation[2] of traditional system boundaries comprises the blurring, erosion, elimination, and washing away of established political, social, and economic boundaries (be these hierarchical or horizontal). Examples include boundaries between high and low culture, education and entertainment, teaching and acting, politics and show business, programs and advertisements, philosophy and literature, fact and fiction, author and reader, science and religion, producer and consumer. It is the dissolution of established distinctions that is captured by terms such as edutainment (an entertaining computer program that is designed to be educational), infomercial (a television show that is an extended advertisement), and docudrama (a drama dealing freely with historical events).

Dedifferentiation and the Web

The Web dissolves perimeters of time, place, and culture. Boundaries between nations, home and work, intimate time and business time, between night and day, and between individuals and organizations. There is no sovereignty in a boundaryless, electronic world. Capital, consumers, and corporations, in the

---

2. Dedifferentiation means the reversion of specialized structures (such as cells) to a more generalized or primitive condition. In contrast, differentiation implies development from the simple to the complex.

form of communication packets, cross political boundaries millions of times every day. We explore two distinctions that the Web is blurring, fact and fantasy, public and private.

First, although hyperreality will be discussed in detail in the next section, it is important to point out that the distinction between reality and virtual reality diminishes on the Web. Fact and fantasy combine, the distinction between representations and their physical form become increasingly blurred. As Web usage increases, and more and more cultural objects are viewed on computer screens, there is likely to be a growing confusion of the representation with the original objects they portray. Amazon.com, promoted as the world's largest bookstore, stocks a few best-sellers. The Web site is the defining presence. The reality is created not by bricks, mortar, and paper, but by digitized fragments displayed on a computer screen.

An example from the Web that illustrates this, and also the resulting blurring of the distinction between high and low culture, is Le MusÈe Imaginaire. Le MusÈe Imaginaire sells paintings by the world's most famous artists such as Van Gogh, Canaletto, and Turner, to the world's most famous people, such as Arnold Schwarzenegger, Sophia Loren, and Michael Jackson. The irony is that they are all fakes—genuine *authentic* fakes. (This can be taken both ways: the pictures are fakes, as the people who buy them are fakes in the sense of being actors and actresses). The fact that the site has received no less than 15 Web-design or cool site awards is testimony to a cyberculture that values the image equal to, or indeed over and above, the real. Indeed, in exact replication, how can one distinguish the authentic from the fake?

A search engine may return 10,000 hits on Shakespeare, but cannot tell you which sites contain genuine content written by the Bard, which contain informed discussion of his works, or which are complete nonsense. This echoes the widespread problem in cyberspace of establishing authenticity and, indeed, questions the very notion of our prior conceptual distinctions. When everything is a re-presentation, how can one speak of an original?

The distinction between private and public is also rendered especially problematic on the Web. All activity (personal and commercial) in cyberspace is routinely monitored to a degree unimaginable in the physical world. A person's activities can be, and routinely are, catalogued in minute detail, and used to build intimate and revealing profiles of that person. People remain ambivalent to this monitoring, for on the one hand, it can help in channeling products and services that have added value to the individual, while on the other, it can represent a flagrant breach of a person's privacy.

In summary, the Web blurs the distinction between private and public in such a way as to make it difficult to compartmentalize our lives in the same way as in the physical world.

Hyperreality

Hyperreality occurs wherein the artifact is even better than the real thing. In a three-stage process, we have (1) the *real* original, (2) the image of the original, and (3) the image uncoupled and freed from the *real* original. Examples include the fantasy world of theme parks (Disneyland), virtual reality (role-playing MUDs, MOOs and GMUKs[3]), situation comedies (*Third Rock from the Sun*), films (*The Lost World*), and computer games (*Myst*). These are examples of what was previously considered a simulation or reflection becoming real—indeed, more real than the real thing. Hyperreality provokes a general loss of the sense of authenticity—i.e., what is genuine, real, or original.

Hyperreality and the Web

The Web is hyperreality. Surfers experience telepresence—the extent to which persons feel present in the hypermedia environment of the Web—when they enter states of high flow. During periods of high flow, time stands still, energy is boundless, and action is effortless. The Web surfer is at one with the Internet, in the same sense that an ocean surfer can get totally immersed in a wave. Thus, surfing is an apt metaphor for describing sustained Web browsing.

Telepresence and flow can lead to addictive surfing, where the normal world is rejected in favor of the virtual, and often fantasy world, of the Web. For example, PJC Ventures is selling plots of land via the Web for $9.95 (€9) for 100 acres. Nothing particularly hyperreal, other than possibly the low price, until one finds out that the plots are on Mars, Pluto, and the other planets! The detachment from reality becomes even more extreme in the face of the U.S. Supreme Court's ruling and the 1967 Multilateral treaty specifying that no person or country can own any part of space. Despite this, some 1,000 plots of land have been sold on Mars and a further 13,000 on the Moon.

The sense of hyperreality is magnified as it becomes increasing difficult to distinguish between genuine and spoof sites (e.g., Microsnot vs. Microsoft), and between professional (run by qualified practitioners) and amateur (run by unqualified enthusiasts) sites (e.g., *British Medical Journal* vs. Dr. Mom). Digital images can be, and are, seamlessly modified. Consider the site Hillary's Hair, which allows surfers to view a vast range of pictures of the First Lady sporting various hairstyles, ranging from the elegant to the very unflattering.

A more dramatic illustration of the hyperreal world created by the Web is the case of bots or intelligent agents, which are autonomous, humanlike computer programs that can help in a variety of tasks. Bots can maintain and optimize your computer, navigate through a complex on-line file structure, and advise players in MUDs, MOOs, etc. Bots are virtual creations designed to pass as

---

3. A GMUK (Graphical multiuser konversations or *habitats*) is a multimedia chat environment, and effectively comprises a cross between a MOO and a chat room.

human beings. As the sophistication of these agents increases, people have been observed to develop emotional relationships with these bots, often unaware that they are virtual creations. However, perhaps even more importantly, those who are aware that these agents are virtual, still find themselves emotionally engaged and treat them as real people.

The case of Julia, an agent of the Mass-Neotek family of robots, has been documented by Foner [1993], who recalls people's attitudes towards, treatment of, and emotional involvement, with the robot as a real person. Furthermore, he reproduces the log of an amusing, yet faintly troubling series of exchanges, covering a 13-day period, between Julia and a love-smitten suitor called "Barry" (name changed), who was blissfully unaware of her virtuality. As Foner wryly observes, it was not entirely clear whether Julia had passed a Turing test[4] or Barry had failed one.

In conclusion, the Web represents a new context where human agents are replaced with virtual agents, and reality is superseded by hyperreality.

Turning fantasy into figures

The tremendous popularity of Fantasy Sports is generating millions of dollars in revenue for Web sites such as ESPN.com and CBS Sportsline. The notion of Fantasy Sports is that a group of people band together and sign on to a virtual sports league by drafting a team based on professional players. The players' statistics are used to generate points, and the winning team is awarded a prize. The cost of a game varies from around $19.95 to $29.95 (€18 to €27).

Because people have invested money in their team, they log onto the Web site regularly to check the scores. The success of Fantasy Sports lies in new people signing up and in the repeat visits they make.

It is estimated that there are over 11 million participants, mostly males in the 18-45 age range with good incomes. This creates tremendous marketing opportunities for the Web sites.

Fitzgerald, M.1999. Pay to play. *Business 2.0*, April 26-27.

Time and space

In the postmodern world, there has been a shift from the standard of linear progress, where the future is always something better than the past, to a model of circularity, where the past is continually recycled, reused, reinterpreted, and

---

4. A Turing test, originally conceived by the mathematician Alan Turing, is a test of whether a computer can pass as being human to another human.

reinvented. Similarly, our experience of space has changed—the world has become a village and the universe, a microverse. These changes portray a general collapse and fragmentation of time and space.

Time and space on the Web

Cyberspace is not a matter of place, but the instant, the eternal present, where pasts and futures are continually recycled in eternal replication. In the computer world of the Web, the physical real is digitized and the digital becomes the real.

Electronic speed has fueled and facilitated the collapsing of space and time in all media. Many traditional media are unable to keep up. Thus, products are often out of date before the consumer gets them home: clothes, software, newspapers, and magazines (the news and weather are now reported immediately on the Web and render many newspapers out of date and irrelevant). In contrast, on the Web the only real currency is the current. For example, one of the authors recently brought the latest version of Norton Anti-Virus, only to be confronted, on loading the software, with the warning that the virus library used to identify malicious code was out of date. However, the program also offered to download the latest library via the Web. This principle is taken one stage further by an innovative piece of software, Oil Change, which allows a person's computer to automatically update its software via the Web the instant an upgrade becomes available. It also undoes any changes so that the user can work with previous versions of the software if he or she chooses.

The Web enables on-line, 24-hour, 365-day buying, selling, and consuming, with real-time delivery of certain products, services, and software. The Web facilitates the decoupling of local time and local space, the desynchronization of local schedules, and the synchronization of global ones. Thus, a wired person can work or teach a class simultaneously in Paris, New York, and Tokyo—while living in the Alps.

The two sides of postmodern time, desynchronization and synchronization, are particularly apparent in cyberspace. On the one hand, the Web is the ultimate source of instant gratification, while on the other, the Web is the ultimate titillation, where gratification is always deferred—one click, one instant, one hypertext link away. The Web feeds desire's ultimate object, desire. This may explain the addictive, drug-like nature of the cyberspace commented on in many magazines and newspapers. Surfing the Web echoes the all-consuming board-surfers' search for the perfect wave.

Fragmentation and digitization of time and space allow recombination into novel configurations that surpass the traditional limitations of space and time. Thus, the Web is facilitating an explosion of virtual companies: teleworking (where distance is negated) replaces local-working (where space and distance predominate—i.e., commuting distance, physical location, quality of the physical offices, etc.).

The U.K.-based Internet Shopper Ltd. is run entirely through Web-mediated teleworking, boasting a staff of some 20, all of whom work from home. Employees are based all over the U.K., from the South East Coast to the Scottish Highlands. All staff were hired over the Internet, work via the Internet, socialize via the Internet (many of the staff have never met face to face), and find their next job via the Internet. Products are developed, refined, sold, and supported via the Internet. In this case, teleworking has dramatically changed working patterns. Employees can structure their days as they please, working when it suits them rather than when one is traditionally expected to be at work. Furthermore, the distinction between work and holiday is becoming increasingly blurred, with employees working via cell phones while basking on the beach.

Finally, the Web is also the ultimate source of endless recycling, replaying, and re-editing of the past. Consider retro-software and retro-computer sites, where one can relive the earliest versions of space invaders, or run your favorite Sinclair ZX spectrum program. Furthermore, because all communication can be recorded on the Web, it is possible for people to relive on-line relationships at any time. Alexa is creating an Archive of the Web for pages that are no longer available. You can relive your favorite Web site of 1996, even though it was erased a year ago.

Paradox, reflexivity, and pastiche

Postmodernism values the other, the paradox (literally that which is beyond belief), the eccentric (that which is out from the center—the decentered). Thus, the theme here is the questioning, and at times active sabotage, of the normal, the orthodox, the stable, and the consistent. It appears as the active seeking of the abnormal, the paradoxical, the dysfunctional, and the excluded. It is the active embracing of the other—indeed, of others.

On the creative side, paradox and reflexivity are actively employed in pastiche.[5] This comprises an often colorful, tongue-in-cheek collage style, or an ironic, self-referential mixing of codes (be these theoretical, philosophical, architectural, artistic, cinematic, literary, musical, etc.).

Paradox, reflexivity, pastiche and the Web

The Web embodies the dual nature of contemporary social phenomena. Duality means that many contemporary social phenomena are not experienced in a simple, unitary, fashion, but as two, often contradictory, parts. Thus, for example, the Web is experienced as both a liberator (it can liberate people from the confines of traditional time and space) and tyrant (it can be addictive,

---

5. A musical, literary, or artistic composition made up of selections from different works.

encouraging compulsive behavior and alienation). It is both constructed (people build Web sites, participate in discussion groups, and shape the way the Web evolves, etc.) and constructor (the Web changes the way we interact and the way in which we construct and experience phenomena—including ourselves).

Computer viruses and hackers also illustrate the duality of the Web. On the one hand, hackers routinely indulge in seemingly malicious destructive activity, while on the other hand, they actively promote the free flow of information. They are reflexively coupled to the world they oppose—the more they hack and create viruses, they more people try to protect themselves and their information. As a result, an ecology has developed in which anti-virus and security software programmers become dependent on the hackers, the parasites, for their existence—the parasites have their parasites.

Consider the phenomena of avatars used in MOOs and GMUKs. Avatars[6] typically refer to pictures (photos, drawings, and cartoons) or graphical objects that people use to represent themselves in cyberhabitats. They can be swapped or modified at will and, in some cases, even stolen. For the point of this discussion, it is interesting to observe that they both reveal and conceal. They can selectively amplify or hide an aspect of a person's character, as well as allow a person to gain experiences outside his or her everyday self.

Finally, most Web sites exemplify pastiche. Styles and themes are borrowed (literally—HTML and JavaScript are routinely lifted from other sites) and mixed freely. Spoof sites, which parody other (typically mainstream) sites, are common (e.g., there are many spoof, irreverent "Spice Girl" sites).

Anti-foundationalism

Anti-foundationalism is a general antipathy towards and rejection of the establishment and orthodoxy. There is a distaste for conforming to doctrines or practices that are held to be right or true by an authority, standard, or tradition. Anti-foundationalism also means a general disbelief of theories, philosophies, or political systems that claim to offer universal goals, rules, truths, or knowledge—and the social institutions that claim to produce them. Examples of these include communism and capitalism and many other social, religious, political, and scientific grand theories.

Anti-foundationalism and the Web

The Web embodies the anti-foundational philosophy of postmodernism in a number of ways. First, the model upon which the Web is based is not the traditional one-to-many of traditional broadcast media, but a many-to-many model in which no one controls the message. Second, the Web effectively has no

---

6. An incarnation in human form.

Cybertextbook

A medical textbook is now available on-line but not through the traditional publishers in that field. Emedicine.com, a company formed by a group of physicians, allows free access to its textbook *Emedicine: emergency medicine*, which would normally retail from $50 to $100 (€45 to €91).

The advantages of this on-line textbook are many: contributions from 400 authors, the information is constantly updated, both audio and video are included, and there is no charge for accessing the information. Sponsorship is provided through corporate and banner advertising, and this medium has tremendous potential.

There are some negatives to consider. Less than 10 percent of physicians and hospital employees have access to the Internet, and are in the habit of referring to hard copy texts. Because the Web site is sponsored by advertising, the book may be perceived as biased towards those advertisers. Also, with many authors having access to the site to update the information, security is a major concern.

Adapted from Cole-Gomolski, B. 1998. Doctors publish cybertextbook. *Computerworld*, Nov. 30, 6.

controlling center or hierarchy. The medium is radically decentered. Nobody controls the Internet.[7] Third, the medium is not stable. It is evolving at an unprecedented rate and in unpredictable directions. The ground is always in motion. There is no foundational control and no one architect; rather, the Web is created by the millions of interactions of all its members.

The logic of the Web is quite different from that of the physical, linear world. The Web is hypertext and hypermedia. It is free of the constraints of traditional writing. A hypermedium is not a closed work with a stable meaning, but an open fabric of links that are in the process of constant revision and supplementation. The traditional author's voice is undermined, and the traditional relationship between author and reader is overthrown. Each reader creates his or her own text and own meaning.

---

7. Although any one body or organization does not control the Web, there are certain players who perform pivotal administrative roles. For example, Network Solutions (www.netsol.com) controls top-level domains. However, due to downloading corrupt zone files on July 18, 1997, to other ISPs (Internet service providers), there are widespread and vociferous calls for the process to be decentralized.

Not surprisingly, the issue of copyright and intellectual property law has become a major issue on the Web. Sites like Total News manage to use other news providers' proprietary content for their own ends while avoiding a breach of copyright laws. The manipulation, editing, threading, and recombination of text, images, sound, and video are fashionable on the Web.

In the fastest growing segments of MOOs and GMUKs there is no game or competition, other than spontaneous role playing and symbolic exchange. In short, there is no overall purpose or goal, no rules or regulation. Individuals create their own rules, reasons, and relations—none is prespecified.

Conclusion

In the modern hi-tech world, there is an ongoing elimination of the distinction between psyche and the environment, between waking and dreaming, between the conscious and the subconscious. When these important boundaries are blurred, people start to lose a sense of themselves. We argue that the Web dramatically speeds up this process. Cyberspace embodies the sudden, hyperreal dynamics of the dream. The conventional rules of time, space, logic, and identity are suspended. The surrealism, simultaneity, and instantaneous change that occur in the dream are embodied in the Web

The Web is rapidly becoming the major medium through which people communicate, make decisions, and even construct their social identities. For some organizations (e.g., Amazon.com and CDNow), the Web is already the dominant forum for business transactions. Making sense of the Web, to the extent that postmodernism facilitates this comprehension, will be essential for insightful organizational practice. The Information Age organization and its stakeholders inhabit the Web. Business research fields (such as consumer behavior, organizational design, and information systems) are based on investigations of corporations and stakeholders interacting in North American Industrial Age settings. The Web eradicates much of this theory, just as the disintegration of the Soviet Union swept away established foreign policy. Now, we need to develop theories of management that incorporate national culture and a networked cybersociety. Postmodernist thinking is a stimulus for fashioning new theories of management and business practice.

The Web confronts modernism because it is a major shift that shakes the very foundation of established management thought. The dominance of broadcast (push technology) has been usurped by the Web (pull technology), and the receiver has taken control from the sender of the timing and content of messages. In the world of advertising, the control of time and space has shifted hands. The trend to decustomize service has been reversed as the Web facilitates mass customization (see page 52). Services are being fragmented to support one-to-one interaction. New firms, the anti-foundationalists, can threaten the establishment within months of their birth (e.g., Netscape threatened Microsoft, and Amazon.com is still a major threat to Barnes &

Noble). Understanding postmodernism is not an easy task, but then again, understanding the consequences of the Web is a major intellectual challenge. Reflecting on postmodernism and its themes should help managers make sense of this new cybersociety.

Cases

De Meyer, A., S. Dutta, and L. Demeester. 1998. *Celebrity sightings.* Fontainebleau, France: INSEA. ECCH 398-074-1.

Dutta, S., A. De Meyer, and P. Evrard. 1997. *LOT Polish airlines & the Internet: flying high in cyberspace.* Fontainebleau, France: INSEAD. ECCH 698-031-1.

References

Csikszentmihalyi, M. 1990. *Flow: the psychology of optimal experience.* New York: Harper & Row.

Foner, L.N. 1993. What's an agent anyway? A sociological case study. May, Agents Group, MIT Media Laboratory.

Hoffman, D. L., and T. P. Novak. 1996. Marketing in hypermedia computer-mediated environments: conceptual foundations. *Journal of Marketing* 60 (July): 50-68.

Glossary

Access control. Techniques for controlling access to stored data or computer resources.

Acquisition. The second stage of the customer service life cycle during which the supplier helps the customer acquire a product or service.

Adaptable Web site. A site that can be customized by the visitor.

Adaptive Web site. A site that learns from the visitor's behavior and determines what should be presented.

Agent. See Intelligent agent.

Anonymous FTP. An FTP site that does not require a user ID and password.

ANSI X12. The ANSI X12 standards specify the format and data content of electronic business transactions.

Attractability efficiency. Measures how effective an organization is in attracting aware people to its Web site.

Attractor. A Web site that continually attracts a high number of visitors.

Authentication. The process of confirming the identity of a person or source of a message.

Awareness efficiency. Measures how effective an organization is in making those with Web access aware of its site.

Backbone. In a computer network, the primary high-speed communications link between major computer centers to which other networks are connected.

Bandwidth. The term used as a measure of the capacity of a communication channel, expressed in bits per second.

Banner. An advertisement that usually covers the bottom or top of a Web page.

Bot. (short for 'robot') A program that operates as an agent for a user or another program or simulates a human activity.

Browser. Client software used on the Web to fetch and read documents on-screen and print them, jump to other documents via hypertext, view images, and listen to audio files.

Business service. The software layer of electronic commerce that handles services required to support business transactions (e.g., encryption).

Centralized computer network. One in which there is one computer or a group of computers to which all other computers must be linked.

Client. A personal computer running an application that can access and display information on a server.

151

Client/server computing. A combination of clients and servers that provides the framework for distributing files across a network.

Codification. An organized method for storing data in a computer system.

Communication flip-flop. A fundamental change in the nature of the relationship between buyers and servers caused by electronic commerce.

Computer network. An interconnected system of computers.

Contact efficiency. Measures how effectively the organization transforms Web site hits into visits.

Conversion efficiency. Measures how effective an organization is in converting visitors into customers who place orders.

Credit card. A safe, secure, and widely used remote payment system.

Customer convergence. The Web marketing concept that firms must describe their products and services so that potential customers converge on the relevant Web pages.

Customer service life cycle. A model that delineates the service relationship with a customer into four phases: requirements, acquisition, ownership, and retirement.

Cyberspace. Another name for the Internet and other forms of electronic communication.

Data access control. A method of controlling access to stored data.

Decentralized computer network. One in which there is no single computer or group of computers to which every other computer is linked.

Decryption. Conversion of encrypted text represented by characters into a readable form.

Demand risk. The risk that changing demand or the collapse of markets significantly reduces demand for a firm's products or services.

Digital cash or money. An electronic form of money that is parallel to notes and coins.

Discussion list. A group of e-mail users who have all subscribed to a listserv to share their ideas on a particular topic.

Distribution. A measure of how widely information is shared.

Divisibility. The extent to which a currency can be divided into small units.

Domain name. Another name for the server computer address.

DNS (domain name service). A system that keeps up with all Internet addresses.

Download. The process of moving software or data from a central computer to a personal computer and saving it on disk.

Ecash. An electronic payment system that can be used to withdraw and deposit ecash over the Internet. It provides the privacy of cash because the payer can remain anonymous.

EDIFACT (EDI for administration, commerce, and transport). United Nations rules for EDI. It comprises a set of internationally agreed upon standards, directories and guidelines for the electronic interchange of structured data related to trade in goods and services between independent computerized information systems.

Electronic commerce. Interacting with stakeholders over computer networks.

Electronic commerce application. A computer interface between an organization and a stakeholder that is used to conduct transactions electronically.

Electronic commerce topology. The three types of communication networks used for electronic commerce: Internet, Intranet, and Interchain.

Electronic communities. Communities that are real in the sense that they are made of people, but electronic in the sense that all communication is in an electronic form.

EDI (Electronic data interchange). The electronic exchange of standard business documents between business partners.

Electronic document. An electronic form of a printed document.

EFT (Electronic funds transfer). The electronic movement of money.

Electronic mail (e-mail). An electronic technology that handles the sending and receiving of messages.

Electronic publishing. The electronic presentation of text and multimedia.

Encryption. The conversion of readable text into characters that disguise the original meaning of the text.

Extranet. An electronic connection using Internet technology linking business partners to facilitate greater coordination of common activities.

File protocol. The Web protocol used to access a local file.

File transfer protocol (FTP). A protocol that supports file transfers over the Internet.

Firewall. A device placed between an organization's network and the Internet to control data access.

Frame. A section of the browser window in which a Web page can be displayed.

FAQs (frequently asked questions). A list of frequently asked questions about software or Web topics along with answers to the questions.

GUI (graphical user interface). An interface that uses pictures and graphic symbols to represent commands, choices, or actions.

Helper application. Software packages linked to the browser in such a way that they are invoked automatically when the user requests that an audio or video file be played or a large image is displayed.

Host computer. A computer in a network that is connected to the Internet.

Hypermedia. An extension of hypertext that includes graphics, video, sound, and music.

Hypertext. A method of linking related information in which there is no hierarchy or menu system.

Hypertext links. Links to other Web pages or Internet resources.

HTML (Hypertext markup language). A markup language used to create Web pages consisting of text, hypertext links, and multimedia elements.

HTTP (hypertext transfer protocol). The protocol for moving hypertext files across the Internet.

Inefficiency risk. The risk that a firm loses market share because it fails to match competitors' unit costs.

Influence filter. A method of making a Web site more attractive to stakeholders.

Information intensity. The degree of information required to describe completely a product or service.

Innovation risk. The risk that a firm fails to continually improve its products and services and loses market share to more innovative competitors.

I²M (integrated Internet marketing). The coordination of Internet facilities to market products and services, shape stakeholder attitudes, and establish or maintain a corporate image.

Intelligent agent. A program that gathers information or performs some other service without your immediate presence and on some regular schedule.

Internet. A worldwide network of computers and computer networks in private organizations, government institutions, and universities, over which people share files, send electronic messages, and have access to vast quantities of information.

Internet newsgroups. See **newsgroups**.

Internet operations. A variety of operations that can be carried out on the Internet including FTP, e-mail, telnet, newsgroups, and the World Wide Web.

Internet service providers. Companies that specialize in linking organizations and individuals to the Internet as well as providing services to them.

Intranet. An intra-organizational network based on using Internet technology. It enables people within the organization to communicate and cooperate with each other.

Java. A platform-independent, object-oriented application development language.

JavaScript. An object-based scripting language for client- and server-side application development. Useful for input validation.

Listserver. A program providing a set of e-mail functions that enables users to participate in electronic discussions.

LAN (local area network). A computer network that is restricted to one geographical area.

Many-to-many communication. A form of communication in which many people can communicate with many other persons.

Market segmentation. The division of a market into segments based on demographic or other relevant variables in order to deliver more precisely an appropriate message to potential customers.

Markup language. A publishing industry term for describing the size, style, and position of each typographical element on a page.

Mass marketing. Broadcasting the same message to all potential customers.

Message distribution. The software layer of electronic commerce that sends and receives messages.

Modem. A communications device that modulates computer signals into outgoing audio signals and demodulates incoming audio signals into computer signals.

Multimedia. An interactive combination of text, graphics, animation, images, audio, and video displayed by and under the control of a personal computer.

Multimedia files. Digitized images, videos, and sound that can be retrieved and converted into an appropriate human recognizable information by a client.

MIME (multipurpose internet mail extension). A protocol that is a widely used for the interchange of files.

MUD (multi-user dimension or dungeon). A multiple-user electronic game that is an ongoing drama with an electronically assembled cast exploring and interacting in cyberspace.

National information infrastructure. A nation's communication networks, including the TV and radio broadcast industries, cable TV, telephone networks, cellular communication systems, computer networks, and the Internet.

Newsgroups. A vast set of Internet discussion lists.

One-to-one marketing. Delivering a specific message to a particular customer, often assisted by a marketing database.

Ownership. The third stage of the customer service life cycle during which the supplier helps the customer maintain a product or service.

Page. An electronic document on the Web that contains text and hypertext links to multimedia elements and other pages that are stored on server computers.

Plug-in. An extension that provides seamless support for data types not supported by the browser.

Point and click navigation. A method that involves using a mouse to position the pointer over a hypertext link or menu bar and clicking a button to retrieve a Web page or execute a command.

Point and click operations. Operations that can be carried out simply by pointing at menu selections or icons representing operations and clicking the mouse button.

PDF (portable document format). A form of electronic document created with Adobe's Acrobat Exchange that can be easily shared with anyone who has an Acrobat reader.

Private key. An encryption key that is known only by the person sending and receiving encrypted messages.

Protocol. A formal set of rules for specifying the format and relationships when exchanging information between communicating devices.

Public key. An encryption key that is known to all persons who share encrypted communication with a particular person (who holds a private key).

Requirements. The first stage of the customer service life cycle during which the supplier helps the customer determine the attributes of the required product or service.

Retention efficiency. Measures how effective an organization is in getting customers to keep ordering.

Retirement. The fourth and final stage of the customer service life cycle during which the supplier helps the customer dispose of a product or service.

Routing. The process of determining the path a message will take from the sending to the receiving computer.

Search engines. Software that has been developed to enable Web users to search for Web pages that contain desired topics.

Secure server. A Web server that provides users protection from having their messages read while being transmitted over the Internet.

Security. The process of protecting stored data and transported messages.

Server. A computer on the Web running an application that manages a data store containing files of text, images, video clips, and sound.

Server address. The address of the computer on which a Web resource is stored.

Service resource. Another name for a protocol on the Web.

SET (secure electronic transaction). A system for ensuring the security of Internet financial transactions.

SGML (standard generalized markup language). A standard that defines a language for document representation which formalizes markup and frees it of system and processing dependencies. It provides a coherent and unambiguous syntax for describing whatever a user chooses to identify within a document.

Shopbot. A program that shops the Web on the customer's behalf and locates the best price for the sought product.

Signed message. A message that can be authenticated as being from a particular person.

Smart card. A card, containing memory and a microprocessor, that can serve as personal identification, credit card, ATM card, telephone credit card, critical medical information record, and as cash for small transactions.

Sniffer. A network program that hackers use to intercept and reads messages on the Internet.

SSL (secure sockets layer). A program layer created by Netscape for managing the security of message transmissions in a network

Stakeholder. Some person or group that can determine the future of an organization.

Target refractor. A method for customizing a Web site to meet the needs of stakeholders.

TCP/IP (transmission control protocol/internet protocol). The communication protocol of the Internet.

URL (uniform resource locator). A standard means of consistently locating Web pages or other resources no matter where they are stored on the Internet.

Value-added network (VAN). A network that offers services over and above those furnished by common carriers. Often used to support EDI.

Value chain. The chain of business activities in which each activity adds value to the end product or service.

Web directory. A hierarchically structured list of Web pages.

Web page. A special type of document that contains hypertext links to other documents or to various multimedia elements.

Web page address. The Internet address at which a Web page is found.

Web searching. The process of searching for Web pages of interest using a piece of software called a search engine.

Web site. An Internet server on which Web pages are stored.

Web site efficiency. A measure for assessing the efficiency of a Web site.

World Wide Web (WWW). A body of software, a set of protocols, and conventions based on hypertext and multimedia techniques that make the Internet easy for anyone to browse and add contributions.

Index